FERDINAND
Magellan

Candy Gourlay

Illustrations by Tom Knight

Abrams Books for Young Readers
New York

The facts in *Ferdinand Magellan* have been carefully checked and are accurate to the best of our knowledge, but if you spot something you think may be incorrect, please let us know. Some of the passages in this book are actual quotes from the journal of Antonio Pigafetta and from other important people. You'll be able to tell which ones they are by the style of type: *The masters and the captains of the other ships of his company loved him not.*

Library of Congress Control Number 2020935323

ISBN 978-1-4197-4678-9

2020 © as UK edition. First published in 2020
by David Fickling Books Limited

Printed and bound in U.S.A.
10 9 8 7 6 5 4 3 2 1

ABRAMS The Art of Books
195 Broadway, New York, NY 10007
abramsbooks.com

CONTENTS

INTRODUCTION

An Unknown Ocean, 1520

Somewhere near Antarctica, three bashed-up ships were sailing wearily into a humongous ocean.

Everyone rushed up on deck. The captain of the expedition took several deep breaths of the salty air— it smelled a lot cleaner than the men. They hadn't bathed for more than a year!

Four hundred and thirty-five days ago, the ships had set off from Spain. They'd crossed the Atlantic Ocean (which was known as the Ocean Sea in those days), stopped in Brazil, and sailed south along the coast until they had come to a sea passage, also called a strait.

They'd entered the strait even though the men were terrified. Nobody had sailed this way before. What had followed was horrible—not just freezing temperatures and wild seas, but conditions that were so challenging that one of their ships turned around and headed back to Spain.

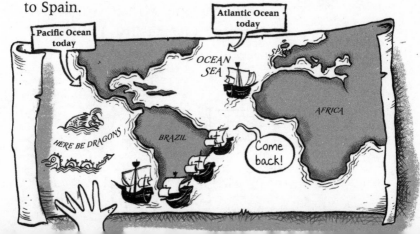

But now, finally, they had come out the other side to find themselves in a new and mysterious ocean.

The captain's name was Ferdinand Magellan. He smiled when he saw how his crew were gaping, their mouths open so wide he could see that their back teeth were blackened from lack of cleaning. This ocean wasn't on any map in 1520—and some of the crew were convinced that giant sea monsters awaited them.

But Ferdinand thought they should be proud. Even Columbus hadn't sailed as far as this splendid blue ocean, which was as smooth as a newly made bed. So calm. So . . . PACIFIC!

That's it! That's what he'd call it. He spread his arms wide. Centuries from now, he, Ferdinand Magellan, would be remembered as the first man to sail the Pacific Ocean!

FIRST? Hang on, we already lived there!

Fair enough! Perhaps we should say Ferdinand Magellan was the first EUROPEAN to sail the Pacific Ocean?

What about us? We were there! We discovered it too!

Today Ferdinand is recognized as one of the greatest explorers ever. He and his fleet "discovered" new animals, the horrible sea passage they'd just left behind, a whole ocean, and even a couple of galaxies.

But, most of all, Ferdinand is remembered as **the first man to sail around the world**.

Did he, or didn't he?

1   FERDINAND'S EARLY DAYS

Ferdinand was born in 1480, surrounded not by rolling waves, as you might expect, but by rolling green vineyards—in Sabrosa, a hilly town in Portugal. He had an older brother, Diogo, and a younger sister, Isabel.

We don't know much about Ferdinand's childhood, but we do know that **the medieval world he was born into was a bit of a mess**. Christians and Moors were at each other's throats.

Countries were constantly at war with each other, and in Portugal the king's own noblemen were plotting against him.

BORN TO BE NOBLE

Ferdinand was lucky enough to be born a member of the nobility—the richest and most powerful people in the land—but only just barely. Being "noble" was all about who your family were. Ferdinand's mom, Alda de Mesquita, had noble relations. His dad, Rodrigo, was related to a famous French knight and was a distant cousin to one of Portugal's most powerful clans: the de Sousa family.

To make absolutely sure nobody could forget the family's connections, Ferdinand's older brother, Diogo, was given the last name de Sousa, instead of Magellan.

By the time Ferdinand was eight or nine, his family had moved to Porto, right on the Atlantic Ocean. His dad had a job in Aveiro, a quiet fishing town nearby. Because of the family's noble connections, Rodrigo Magellan expected that his sons would someday become **pages at the royal court in Lisbon** . . .

SUGAR AND SPICE

Life in Porto was comfortable enough, but the food was incredibly boring. It was the Middle Ages, so no one in Europe had ever tasted avocados, peppers, potatoes, or tomatoes, and **there was definitely no chocolate**!

Nobles like me ate with spoons, knives, and our fingers off trenchers—round, flat loaves of bread cut in half and used as plates.

In Ferdinand's day, spices such as pepper, cinnamon, cloves, and nutmeg were used for many things. Rich people used them to flavor their food. They thought the spices helped their digestion and had healing properties. People also believed diseases were carried in the air and smelling spices would protect them.

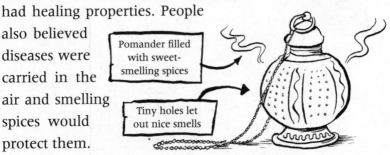

Pomander filled with sweet-smelling spices

Tiny holes let out nice smells

But **spices were expensive**. They came from faraway Asia and could only be bought from Arab merchants who traded them in Egypt and Syria.

But rich people didn't mind the cost. They liked showing off!

But then there was a crisis: **The spices stopped coming.**

Here's where the spices had been coming from:

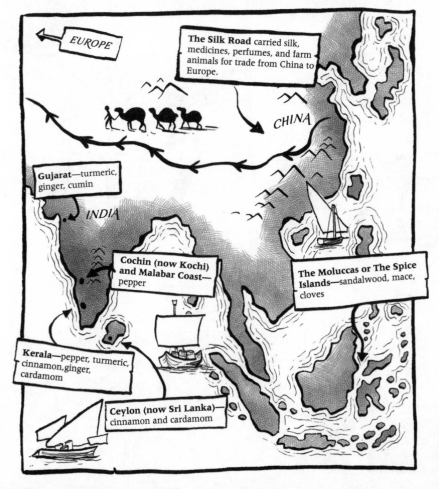

EUROPE

The **Silk Road** carried silk, medicines, perfumes, and farm animals for trade from China to Europe.

CHINA

Gujarat—turmeric, ginger, cumin

INDIA

Cochin (now Kochi) and Malabar Coast—pepper

The Moluccas or The Spice Islands—sandalwood, mace, cloves

Kerala—pepper, turmeric, cinnamon, ginger, cardamom

Ceylon (now Sri Lanka)—cinnamon and cardamom

FERDINAND EXPLAINS: THE SPICE TRADE

More than a thousand years before I was born, Arab sailors began trading spices they brought from India and the East Indies (that's Southeast Asia today).

The sailors didn't want their customers to know where the spices came from—what if they went off to buy their own? So, they frightened their clients with tall tales:

And then the giant birds carry cattle to their nests and the cinnamon falls to the ground for people to collect.

Eek! Better you than me.

The ancient Greeks and Romans traded with the Arabs, taking the spices across their empires, which was how Europeans first got a taste for them.

How much to add the rug?

During the Middle Ages, the city of Venice became the hotspot for European trade. It was very friendly with the city of Constantinople, (now known as Istanbul in Turkey), where Venetian merchants made lots of money trading with Arabs for spices and luxury goods like silk, ivory, porcelain, gold, and silver.

Hi Yusuf! How's the wife?

But Constantinople was slowly losing territory to the Ottoman Empire. By 1453, the Ottomans had taken over. Soon they controlled Egypt and the Red Sea, blocking all trade with Christians. The result: no more spices for Europe.

TRADE ROUTE CLOSED

Which is how the Age of Exploration began . . .

If we cannot get the spices by land, we will send explorers to find a route so we can get them by sea!

Suddenly, Portugal and the rest of Europe were in a race to find a sea route to Asia—and the Spice Islands.

FERDINAND BEGINS TO DREAM

The river Douro wound through the city of Porto like a fat snake before emptying into the Atlantic Ocean. Wherever Ferdinand was in Porto, he could see all kinds of vessels traveling up and down the river, among them caravels with their sleek, triangular sails and carracks with their boxy sails. These were **the ships of explorers**! They were state of the art and able to sail long distances.

Caravel

Carrack

King John's explorers hadn't found a sea passage to Asia yet, but Ferdinand was certain it was only a matter of time—**Portugal had the best sailors in the world**!

Already, the ships that the king had sent east were returning from Africa and introducing new and marvelous goods to the city. Ferdinand could hear the crackle of foreign tongues everywhere and see men of all races striding along the cobbled streets, and he was filled with longing. Could a boy like him someday become one of King John's explorers? Could he captain his own ship and travel to new and wonderful places?

But just as he was daring to dream such dreams, **catastrophe struck**. In 1490, both his parents died.

I was only ten years old.

2   FERDINAND'S GOOD FORTUNE

It's always horrible to be orphaned, but being orphaned was particularly horrible in Portugal in the Middle Ages. Back then, orphans with no family who could take them in might be:

✸ Handed over to the church or to a monastery, where they'd be treated like servants.

✸ Sent as settlers to newly discovered lands.

✸ Sent to the new lands to marry Portuguese settlers (if they were girls).

Luckily for Ferdinand and Diogo, because they were noble, they were sent to Queen Eleanor's School for Pages in Lisbon (which was very close to all those royals), while their sister, Isabel, was looked after by rich relatives.

FERDINAND EXPLAINS:

QUEEN ELEANOR'S SCHOOL

Only boys from noble families are sent to Queen Eleanor's School for Pages. There, we had to learn . . .

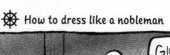 How to dress like a nobleman

Glurk!

 How to dance like a nobleman

No!

 Hawking, riding, and fencing

Yes!

 Algebra, geometry, astronomy, and navigation (my favorite!)

A page's job is to look after courtiers. When we're older, we become squires who help knights dress and get into their armor, and fetch and carry things for them.

I'm too fancy to dress myself!

This isn't my idea of being noble!

We don't really know what Queen Eleanor's School for Pages looked like. But we do know that Ferdinand and his brother went on to serve at the Castle of Saint George, built centuries before, when Portugal was ruled by Moors.

The School for Pages was probably a lot like a **really fancy boarding school**. Ferdinand and Diogo would have had to fit in with boys from some of the wealthiest families in Portugal.

It couldn't have been easy. Ferdinand and Diogo's claim to nobility was distant. Plus, in those days, **people looked down on orphans**. Not only that, it was uncool to come from Porto. People from Porto were known as "tripeiros"—eaters of tripe, which is the lining of cow stomachs!

You Porto people eat cow guts!

Tripas à moda do Porto.* Yum!

We're called tripeiros because in 1415 the people of our city gave all their meat to the king's army, leaving them with nothing but tripe to eat. We're proud of our history!

* Porto tripe stew

At the same age, poorer boys would have worked as apprentices, maybe to blacksmiths, cooks, or winemakers. Being a page was an apprenticeship too, but instead of learning a trade, a page was learning how to act like a rich person.

Ferdinand probably learned a lot more outside of his lessons by watching the stream of explorers who visited King John. They came to tell stories of their adventures—and to beg him to sponsor them.

The king's gold could mean the success or failure of an expedition. Ferdinand soon learned that winning the king's support was all about whether or not the king liked you.

Portugal's knowledge of long-distance navigation was way ahead of its nearest rivals. **Explorers were the rock stars of Ferdinand's era.** No doubt all the boys in Lisbon dreamed of sailing their own ships and discovering their own uncharted territories.

But Ferdinand was luckier than most Lisbon boys, and he knew it. Here he was, learning all the skills he needed to captain his own ship, and serving a king who didn't just believe in exploration but had the gold to make it happen!

Enter Christopher Columbus

One day, in 1493, when Ferdinand was just thirteen, a violent storm blew a ship into Lisbon harbor. It was a caravel. Etched on its barnacle-encrusted side was its name, *La Santa Clara*. It flew the flag of Portugal's fierce rival: Spain.

The king sent one of his top captains, Bartholomew Diaz, to demand what business the ship had with Lisbon. When Diaz returned, his news sent an excited murmur through the crowd that had gathered.

The ship was captained by an Italian sailor named Christopher Columbus. Just a few years earlier, Columbus had approached King John with an outlandish proposition: a voyage to Asia, **not by sailing east but by sailing west** . . . across the Atlantic Ocean.

The idea was ridiculous. Nobody knew what lay across the ocean. The king had kicked Columbus out of the throne room.

But now, here he was again, saying that King Ferdinand and Queen Isabella of Spain had given him the gold to fund his travels, and telling everyone that **his voyage had been a success**. He *had* sailed all the way to the East Indies in Asia. He'd proved, once and for all, that the world was round!

* Their calculations were correct!

It took Columbus ten weeks, but he'd gotten there . . . **Except he hadn't**.

He hadn't been anywhere near the East Indies (which is Indonesia, Malaysia, and the Philippines today). The truth was, Columbus had landed on the Caribbean islands of the Bahamas and Hispaniola. His later journeys took him to South America. Eventually, the lands we call North and South America today became known as the New World.

It was years before people figured out that Columbus had gotten it wrong, and in the meantime King John was **ready to explode** with fury and envy.

He let Columbus go, and then he traveled to Spain and faced off with Spain's two monarchs, Ferdinand and Isabella. In 1479, Spain and Portugal had agreed to a treaty saying that all land discovered south of the Canary Islands belonged to Portugal. John insisted that though the Spanish royals had paid for his trip, all Columbus's discoveries really belonged to Portugal.

But Ferdinand and Isabella weren't going to give in easily. Their bickering got so nasty that they had to call in Pope Alexander VI to settle the argument.

The pope drew a line across the world.

At first, Spain was just happy to avoid a war with Portugal—King John had a far more powerful army. Besides, if any lands discovered to the west of the line belonged to them, then Columbus's discovery was theirs to conquer. Yay!

But they realized too late that **they were probably on the wrong side of the line**. Nobody knew much about what was west of the Canary Islands and they were already beginning to doubt that Columbus had actually reached Asia. On the Portuguese side of the line, though, there was Africa—and most importantly, the Spice Islands.

THE AGE OF EXPLORATION

The Age of Exploration was a time when Europeans began finding lands beyond their own shores. For anyone who already lived in these "new" places, though, it was a time of invasion and occupation.

SPAIN

PORTUGAL

1. PRINCE HENRY THE NAVIGATOR

Portuguese Prince Henry didn't actually do any navigating, but between 1419 and 1460, he sent dozens of expeditions to explore the West African coast. On the plus side, his men kept records of tides, currents, and winds, charting the way for future explorers. But Henry also started the Atlantic Slave Trade when he captured African people and brought them to Portugal to sell.

2. BARTHOLOMEW DIAZ

Europeans knew from travelers and merchants that the Indian Ocean was on the other side of Africa. But for a long time, they didn't have ships that could travel long distances and they didn't understand how the ocean currents could help or hinder their travels. In 1488, Portugal's Bartholomew Diaz became the first European to sail around the southern tip of Africa (known as the Cape of Good Hope today) and enter the waters of the Indian Ocean.

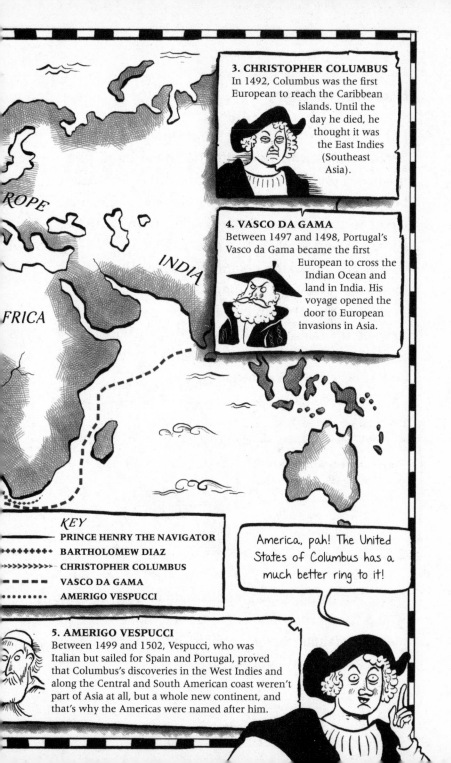

3. CHRISTOPHER COLUMBUS
In 1492, Columbus was the first European to reach the Caribbean islands. Until the day he died, he thought it was the East Indies (Southeast Asia).

4. VASCO DA GAMA
Between 1497 and 1498, Portugal's Vasco da Gama became the first European to cross the Indian Ocean and land in India. His voyage opened the door to European invasions in Asia.

KEY
————— **PRINCE HENRY THE NAVIGATOR**
+++++++++ **BARTHOLOMEW DIAZ**
>>>>>>>>> **CHRISTOPHER COLUMBUS**
— — — — **VASCO DA GAMA**
••••••••• **AMERIGO VESPUCCI**

America, pah! The United States of Columbus has a much better ring to it!

5. AMERIGO VESPUCCI
Between 1499 and 1502, Vespucci, who was Italian but sailed for Spain and Portugal, proved that Columbus's discoveries in the West Indies and along the Central and South American coast weren't part of Asia at all, but a whole new continent, and that's why the Americas were named after him.

Unfortunate News

Columbus's discovery sent King John into a frenzy. **Spain couldn't win!** He would just build more ships, finance more expeditions! Weren't the Portuguese better sailors? Didn't they have the most up-to-date charts in the world and the best sea routes? He was going to show Spain!

And then the king became paranoid. The Spanish had spies everywhere, didn't they? What if they managed to steal his precious maps and charts? Just to be on the safe side, John ordered all the knowledge Portugal had collected about seafaring routes, winds, and tides to be **locked away** and kept secret from the rest of the world.

All discoveries were recorded on a map called the Padrão Real, which was kept far away from any foreign spies and merchants.

The king's obsession spread through Lisbon like a fever. Ferdinand, Diogo, and the other boys at court would have been caught up in it too, hooked on the idea of captaining their own ships, out-exploring Spain, and becoming heroes of Portugal.

But then disaster struck.
In 1495, King John fell
sick . . . and died.

Because John had no legitimate son, he'd recognized the queen's younger brother, Manuel, as his heir. The twenty-six-year-old became King Manuel I.

3 FERDINAND INTO THE FRAY

But King Manuel the Fortunate turned out to be nothing like King John. In fact, Manuel *hated* John because he'd killed so many of Manuel's family! Sure, they'd been plotting to overthrow him . . . but still!

So, the first thing Manuel did once he became king was to **kick John's friends out** of the royal castle. Then he took away their properties and handed them out to his own pals instead.

Imagine how fifteen-year-old Ferdinand felt! He had been one of King John's biggest fans. Would Manuel dismiss him as well?

Manuel didn't send Ferdinand away. But he might as well have, because he only ever gave Ferdinand a hard time in the royal court. All opportunities were given to other people. **Ferdinand was stuck.**

FROM BORING TO SCORING

Ferdinand was desperate to join an expedition, go to sea, discover new places, fight wars! He probably begged and begged for permission to go, but it's clear Manuel said no, because Ferdinand was ordered to take a desk job at the Royal Trading House.

The House supervised ships—both trading ships and explorers' ships. Ferdinand would have had to handle tedious stuff like licensing, taxes, finance, contracts, and scheduling.

On the bright side, the House did work closely with another department, the Armazém—or the Depository—which dealt with the non-boring aspects of shipping. Equipment! Weapons! Navigation! Maps!

Ferdinand was stuck behind a desk for ten long years! Then, in the summer of 1499, his ho-hum existence was interrupted by the arrival of a captain named Vasco da Gama to the Port of Lisbon.

Da Gama had pulled off what no other explorer had managed: **He'd traveled beyond the southern tip of Africa** . . . all the way to India.

FERDINAND EXPLAINS:

VASCO DA GAMA'S VOYAGE

The voyage was King John's idea and King Manuel carried it through.

Da Gama sailed south along the African coast, then swung out into the Atlantic on the westerly winds and looped back to the Cape of Good Hope.

EUROPE

LISBON

AFRICA

INDIA

CALICUT

MALINDI
MOMBASA

MOZAMBIQUE

CAPE OF GOOD HOPE

MOZAMBIQUE, MARCH 2–29, 1498
Da Gama insulted the king by offering cheap gifts, then fired cannons into the city.

MOMBASA, APRIL 7–13, 1498
He met unarmed Arab merchant ships . . . and looted them.

BOOM!

YIKES!

CALICUT, MAY 1498
Three thousand warriors welcomed de Gama, but the king didn't like his gifts.

MALINDI, APRIL 14, 1498
Da Gama met Indians for the first time. They were friendly (because they hadn't heard about the lootings yet).

Red hats? Are you serious?

HOMEWARD BOUND, 1499
Locals told da Gama not to sail for home because of monsoon winds. Da Gama sailed anyway, in horrible storms, against the wind. He only brought back a small amount of spices because he'd taken so many less valuable goods to trade, but he'd made it to India.

It took 23 days to sail to India.

And 132 days to get back. Half his crew died!

Ferdinand had never seen King Manuel so excited. Da Gama was greeted on the harbor by the king's best carriages. Cheering crowds lined the city's steep avenues as the explorer was triumphantly paraded to the castle, where he was honored by the court with lavish feasts and flattering speeches and awarded a new, impressive title by King Manuel: Admiral of the Seas of Arabia, Persia, India, and All of the Orient.

Ha-ha! Take that, king and queen of Spain! The Spice Trade is ours!

Winning isn't everything . . . JUST KIDDING!

The eastern shore of Africa was lined with bustling settlements and small kingdoms that the Portuguese had never heard of before. Da Gama and his crew had expected wild, primitive people and couldn't believe their eyes when they found **sophisticated cultures that had been trading with each other for centuries**. Their amazing bazaars were stocked with spices and exotic goods from India, China, and Southeast Asia—all the stuff that Europe craved.

And most astonishing (and insulting) of all, nobody was dazzled by da Gama's gifts of cloth, hats, brass vessels, sugar, oil, and honey. They were used to much finer stuff—preferably gold and silver.

Listening to da Gama's tales, Manuel realized that if he was going to take control of the Spice Trade, he couldn't just befriend the people on the other side of Africa, because they weren't interested in anything he had to offer. **He'd have to conquer them.**

CONQUERING THE INDIAN OCEAN

The Royal Trading House went into overdrive. Ferdinand would have had a gazillion things to do preparing the ships that would invade the kingdoms da Gama had discovered in the name of King Manuel. By 1504, Manuel had sent six fleets to the Indian Ocean.

⚓ The ships raided settlements on the shores of Africa and India and claimed the land for the king.

⚓ They demanded tributes from local chiefs, and when people fought back, they bombarded them with cannon fire.

⚓ Manuel's fleets crisscrossed the Indian Ocean, attacking and looting unarmed merchant ships. They were especially brutal when it came to their traditional enemy, the Moors. In one incident, da Gama had hundreds of Moors burned to death in their boat.

The whole of Portugal was dazzled by the stories of conquest. The Portuguese couldn't help feeling proud that their little kingdom was building its own empire. Wealth began to pour in. **Spices were back on the menu!** The whole of Europe was filling Portugal's coffers in exchange for spices and other luxury goods the ships were bringing back from Asia. Lisbon was changing right before Ferdinand's eyes, becoming shinier, richer, grander. And the food was smelling pretty good now that there were spices again!

But on the Indian Ocean there was only **death, terror, and destruction**.

Kingdoms around the Indian Ocean discussed what to do about the Portuguese. Even the Venetians joined in—after all, the Portuguese were stealing their trade too. The Mamluk sultan of Egypt began putting together a war fleet. They approached Pope Julius II, threatening at first, but then begging him to make the Portuguese stop their attacks.

Bad idea. When the pope asked King Manuel to calm things down, Manuel flew into a rage.

Manuel assembled twenty-two warships, which was quite a lot back then. He called it the Seventh India Armada.

Manuel had the money to deck them out . . . but did he have enough men? He needed at least 1,500 soldiers, sailors, and other crew members, but many of Portugal's experienced seamen were already out on other expeditions. After a lot of shouting he finally managed it. But he couldn't be picky.

Which meant that when Ferdinand applied to join the Seventh India Armada, Manuel finally forgot about Ferdinand's loyalty to King John and **actually said YES**! It was 1505. Ferdinand found himself on a warship with his brother, Diogo, and a cousin, Francisco Serrão.

Woohoo!

In those days, noblemen could only be ship's officers or passengers. It was unthinkable for a nobleman to become part of the lowly crew or even be **paid to work on a ship** (that would have meant losing their status). Fighting, on the other hand, *was* allowed.

So, Ferdinand, Diogo, and Francisco had to sign up as sobresaliente or "gentlemen adventurers"—noblemen who came for the adventure, not the money.

The armada set to work. Half of the fleet headed for India. The other half, with Ferdinand onboard, terrorized the kingdoms on the African shore, attacking the port of Mombasa, stealing gold, capturing hundreds of slaves, and **killing lots of people**.

Ferdinand threw himself into it all—apparently taking part in the sinking of two hundred ships! The fleet commander, Francisco Almeida, was so impressed that he promoted Ferdinand to assistant captain on one of the caravels!

Almeida even wrote a glowing letter to King Manuel, commending Ferdinand for his courage and leadership. The letter must have filled Ferdinand with hope.

On to India

After two years in Africa, Ferdinand's fleet sailed to India.

The king had promised Commander Almeida that if he could build four fortresses along the western coast of India, he would be declared the viceroy of India—which meant he was basically in charge when the king wasn't around. Almeida only built three forts, then **he declared himself viceroy**!

Meanwhile, King Manuel decided to call himself "Lord of Guinea and of the Navigation and Commerce of Ethiopia, Arabia, Persia, and India."

Then, in 1508, a guy named Afonso Albuquerque turned up in India, saying King Manuel had appointed *him* to take over as viceroy of India! Almeida didn't believe him. He put Albuquerque in jail and continued conquering the country. By 1509, he had worked his way down the coast, clashing with one Indian state after another. **Ferdinand fought with him** the whole way.

The Final Reckoning

Finally, the Moors got a fleet together for a big push against the Portuguese. The Mamluk sultan in Egypt provided soldiers, the Venetians supplied warships, and other fighters from the Ottoman Empire, Gujarat, and Calicut joined in too. But could they beat the battle-hardened Portuguese?

The Battle of Diu, as it became known, took place in the harbor of Diu, in northeast India. It's one of the **most important battles in history**. We don't know exactly what role Ferdinand played, but we do know that the fighting was intense.

Like pesky mosquitoes, small boats harassed the big Portuguese ships.

Ethiopian and Turkish bowmen showered arrows from above.

Ships rammed into each other.

The Portuguese fired their cannons.

Men fought on deck

The Moors tried to attack from behind, but the Portuguese blocked their way with one of their biggest ships. Crammed together in the water below, the Moors were helpless as the Portuguese gunners shot at them from above.

The Battle of Diu decided once and for all who ruled the Indian Ocean. The Moors fled, leaving tiny Portugal to build **one of the biggest empires** the world had ever seen.

4   FERDINAND FRUSTRATED

Ferdinand spent months recovering from his battle wounds in Portuguese India, and when he reported for duty again, he found he had a new commander, a new fleet, and a new mission. After defeating the Moorish alliance and conquering the west coast of India, were the Portuguese ready to relax and begin enjoying the profits of their invasions?

Nope! They still hadn't made it to the Spice Islands.

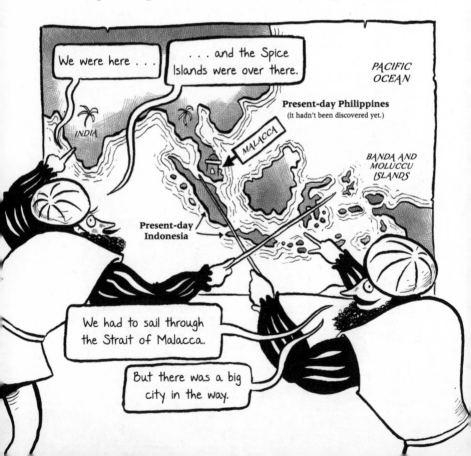

Malacca was a rich city along a strait that led to the Spice Islands. If the Portuguese wanted to reach those islands, they'd have to conquer Malacca.

FRACAS IN MALACCA

Ferdinand's mission was a sneaky one. He joined a small fleet with just five ships and sailed into Malacca. There, the crew pretended to be traders, but they were really spying on the sultan and reporting back to India to plan an attack.

Ferdinand and his men had heard tales of the wealth of Malacca—the dazzling bazaars stocked with precious stones, spices, weaponry, fine fabrics, porcelain, and ivory—but **they weren't prepared for their first sight of the wooden city**. It was dominated by the sultan's spectacular ironwood palace, with its many-tiered, red-shingled roofs that looked like clusters of floating pyramids. An enormous stone mosque loomed nearby. The sea approach was packed with more ships than the Portuguese had ever seen in any harbor.

Gliding into port, they must have wondered how all these people, in their astonishing array of clothing, had come to be here. And how come they all seemed to be getting along so peacefully with each other.

The city seemed friendly and its ruler, Sultan Mahmud, agreed to allow the Portuguese to trade in the city. For a few days, **the crews of the five ships relaxed**. They even did a spot of sightseeing.

One day, Ferdinand's cousin Francisco and a large group of men rowed to shore to stretch their legs and look around. Smaller craft began to surround the ships but nobody took much notice—Malacca's traders were always coming to bargain for the goods that the fake merchants had brought with them. The fleet's commander, Diogo Lopez de Sequeira, left his men to deal with them and sat down to a game of chess on deck. Ferdinand, still sore from his wounds, couldn't help feeling wary—there seemed to be more traders than usual on deck.

Then Ferdinand spotted a glint of steel in the throng. Quietly, he muttered a warning to the captain. De Sequeira had barely registered what Ferdinand said when they saw smoke suddenly streaming above the palace. **It was a signal to attack.**

Suddenly, the traders drew their swords, and Ferdinand and the captain found themselves in the thick of combat. These men weren't traders! **They'd come to seize the ship!**

The Portuguese crew hadn't fooled anyone—of course the Malaccans knew what they were up to! Sultan Mahmud had heard all about the carnage the Portuguese had inflicted on both coasts of the Indian Ocean. He had no plans to allow that to happen to his little kingdom.

RESCUE AND REVENGE

As the fighting intensified, Ferdinand glanced toward the city and saw a large crowd surrounding the Portuguese crew who'd gone ashore. Francisco was in danger!

Ferdinand didn't hesitate. He and another crew member jumped into a boat and rowed to the shore. Some of the Portuguese managed to break away from their attackers, race for the water, and throw themselves into the waiting boat. Luckily, Francisco was one of them, but many men were left behind and taken prisoner.

It was tough but they finally managed to fight off Mahmud's men. The ships weighed anchor and sailed away, leaving some of the crew in the hands of the sultan.

Sultan Mahmud must have been relieved to see the little fleet leave. But two years later, in 1511, the Portuguese came back—with a squadron of nineteen ships, led by India's new viceroy, Afonso Albuquerque, who'd finally convinced Ferdinand's old boss Almeida to step down. This time, it was the sultan who was forced to flee, and **for the next hundred years, Portugal ruled Malacca.**

Meanwhile, a fourteen-year-old boy became Ferdinand's slave in Malacca. We don't know if Ferdinand bought him at a slave market or if the boy was given to Ferdinand as a reward by Albuquerque, but we do know that Ferdinand gave him a Portuguese name: Enrique. And we know that Enrique stayed at Ferdinand's side until Ferdinand died.

Home Sweet Home

In 1513, with Enrique in tow, Ferdinand returned to Portugal. He was thirty-three and he'd been away for eight long years. He was exhausted but proud of his achievements—**there was no doubt that he was a war hero.**

All he wanted to do was go back to the comfort of his home, live on some money he'd carefully invested with a reliable merchant before he'd left the country, and bask in the admiration of the court.

But to Ferdinand's surprise, Lisbon had completely changed while he'd been abroad. People seemed well fed and they were strutting the streets in finery from the Far East. There was scaffolding everywhere, with new churches and monumental architecture popping up all over the city. The new architecture was showy, with lots of fancy carved stonework that had a maritime theme: anchors, chains, ropes, cables, seashells, fish, pearls . . . even strings of seaweed! The plain walls of buildings were covered with fancy ceramic tiling in the style of Moorish architecture he'd seen abroad.

Seeing this made Ferdinand smile. The city was obviously proud of how its new wealth had been won by men like him! The years he'd spent in grueling battles had been worth it. But when Ferdinand visited the house of the merchant he'd entrusted with his investments, he was met with shocking news.

All of Ferdinand's money was gone! Suddenly, his dreams of a break vanished. He hurried to the royal court. Surely someone there would help him. In all the years he'd been abroad, he had fantasized about how the court must be singing his praises and telling stories about his bravery, his injuries, his victories— the way they'd sung the praises of explorers when he'd been a page.

But when he arrived at the castle, there were no familiar faces. **Nobody had any idea who he was** or what he'd done. When he checked his own records at the Royal Trading House, he got yet another shock: He was still listed as a **junior squire**!

WORSE AND WORSE

Dazed, Ferdinand decided he had no choice but to go directly to the king. His commanders had written glowing letters about him. Surely Manuel would help him now.

But when they were face to face, Ferdinand felt a chill run through his veins. The same disdain gleamed in the king's eyes. Nothing had changed—**Manuel still despised him.**

FIGHTING AGAIN

Ferdinand had already seen too much war, but he was desperate for money. There was news of a rebellion in Morocco, and the king's army was looking for volunteers, so Ferdinand signed up.

Things didn't get any better for him though:

- He lost his horse in one battle.

- In another, a Moroccan spear shattered his knee, leaving him with a limp.

- Worse still, his commander appointed him to manage a herd of captured goats.

But that wasn't the worst of it. Ferdinand sold the animals to pay off some locals who had helped him. Big mistake. He found himself in court, accused of **illegal goat trafficking**!

Ferdinand wasn't charged, but instead of staying out of trouble, he bypassed his commander and went straight to King Manuel to demand a pay raise. Manuel was not impressed.

Ferdinand wasn't exactly the most tactful person. He'd annoyed his commander, and now he'd annoyed the king.

LETTERS FROM FRANCISCO

One day, Ferdinand received a letter from his cousin. Francisco had been sent to the Spice Islands. Traders had been few and far between while the Portuguese were making war in the Indian Ocean, and the islanders welcomed him with open arms. Francisco packed his ships full to bursting with spices.

When a storm wrecked his boat, Francisco was rescued by one of the sultans. He loved life on the island so much that he'd married a local and decided to stay.

I have found here a new world richer and greater than that of Vasco da Gama. I beg you to join me here, that you may sample for yourself the delights that surround me.

FERDINAND'S IDEA

While Ferdinand had been away, explorers had spotted an ocean from the mountains of South America. They called it the South Sea.

Hearing the news, Ferdinand began to think. Bartholomew Diaz had found a route from the Atlantic to the Indian Ocean. And he himself had sailed the Strait of Malacca that linked India to the Spice Islands. Surely, if he sailed far enough south, **he would find a way from the Atlantic to the South Sea**.

But *where* did the South Sea lead?

Ferdinand met an astronomer named Rui Faleiro, who claimed he'd already calculated the precise location of a sea passage to the South Sea.

Ferdinand's mind must have been racing. His cousin Francisco was waiting for him on a white sandy beach in the South Sea. Reports had already confirmed that the South Sea was on the other side of the new continent. And Faleiro knew exactly how to sail there.

There was no time to lose. With Faleiro at Ferdinand's side, **Manuel would surely agree** to an expedition!

THE KING SAYS NO

It was as if Ferdinand had forgotten how much Manuel disliked him. He began to pester the king for a private meeting. Manuel *did* agree to meet Ferdinand but on a day that was reserved for peasants! Ferdinand had to wait in line with the commoners, and when he finally got to explain his plan, it didn't go well.

It turned out that the king already knew Faleiro—and not in a good way. Faleiro had applied to become the royal astronomer, and when Manuel chose someone else, Faleiro had thrown a massive temper tantrum. Now, **the king disliked Faleiro even more than he disliked Ferdinand**. How were they ever going to win him over?

When Ferdinand finally secured another meeting with the king, he asked if Manuel would rather they applied to some other royal. The king said yes.

Ferdinand was stunned. As Manuel dismissed him, he knelt to kiss the king's hand (which was the custom), but Manuel hid his hands in his cloak and turned his back.

That was the last straw.

Ferdinand may have been broke, and he may have been injured, but he was a genuine war hero, who had served his king loyally and courageously. If Manuel wasn't interested in his expedition, then **he'd take his idea to the new Spanish king**, Charles I.

That's why, in 1517, Ferdinand and Faleiro both gave up their Portuguese citizenship and left Lisbon for Spain.

5   FERDINAND CHANGES KINGS

King Manuel almost exploded with rage. How dare Ferdinand renounce his king! How dare he leave his country! How dare he side with Portugal's worst enemy! (He must have forgotten that he'd given Ferdinand permission to leave in the first place.)

And then . . . Manuel began to worry. Ferdinand had worked for the Royal Trading House for years. He'd had access to Portugal's greatest seafaring secrets. Clearly, Ferdinand had stolen some of those secrets and would use them to impress the Spanish king!

Well, no way was that scoundrel going to betray Portugal! Manuel would make sure Ferdinand failed with the Spanish, or he'd die trying. He started with Ferdinand's family.

The king had us tear down the family's coat of arms!

We had to smear it with dung!

Actually, Ferdinand didn't think going to another country was unusual. He was just following in the footsteps of other explorers, like Columbus, who sailed for Spain even though he was actually Italian.

WELCOME TO SEVILLE

When Ferdinand arrived in the Spanish city of Seville, **everything looked strangely familiar**.

Like Lisbon, the city rang with the sound of construction. The people of Seville were also building great flashy buildings with the gold their ships had plundered from their explorations. But alongside the grand architecture were squalid slums. The gold (and the opportunities it brought) was also attracting people from all over Spain like bears to honey. The streets thronged with sailors, foreign merchants, and slaves of many races. Windows boasted cages of small yellow birds imported from the Canary Islands—one of Spain's colonies.

But Ferdinand quickly realized that Spain and Portugal had **radically different attitudes to exploration**. While the Portuguese treated exploration like a state secret . . . **the Spanish loved to boast about their exploits**. The printing press had just been invented and the libraries of rich people were well stocked with pamphlets and books about voyages of exploration.

Leaking information is punishable by death!

Even so, Ferdinand was nervous. He didn't know anyone at court, and he wasn't sure how the king would react to a Portuguese captain. But to Ferdinand's surprise, once he reached Seville, **his luck seemed to change**.

First, he befriended a man named Diogo Barbosa who, like Ferdinand, was Portuguese but had switched his allegiance to Spain. Barbosa was rich and well connected, and he became Ferdinand's mentor, teaching him the best tactics to use in approaching the king.

Then, he met Barbosa's daughter Beatriz. Before the year was out, Ferdinand and Beatriz were married.

I, Ferdinand Magellan, will become the greatest explorer on Earth!

You're supposed to say "I do!"

To start with, Ferdinand had to approach the Casa de Contratación—the House of Commerce. It was an agency that vetted proposals to the king.

Ferdinand probably thought he would have to keep bugging them the way he'd had to keep pestering Manuel. But **the Casa seemed friendly**, and a mere three months after arriving in Spain, Ferdinand found himself on his way to the royal residence with an appointment to see King Charles I.

KING CHARLES I

Ferdinand must have been a little bit thrown. The king was, in fact, a peculiar-looking eighteen-year-old boy with a very long chin. What could this young lad possibly know about exploration?

Charles was born in Ghent and had grown up in Belgium. He'd only just moved to Spain to take the throne, so he could barely speak Spanish (just like Ferdinand). But he wasn't just king of Spain: He was heir to three of the top families in Europe and already **had a load of titles and kingdoms**. He was also tipped to become Holy Roman Emperor, ruling over parts of present-day Germany, France, Italy, and eastern Europe . . . but that's another story. Basically, he needed a *lot* of gold to make sure he won that title.

Ferdinand squared his shoulders and set aside his anxieties. He knew **he had to give the performance of his life**, and what a performance he'd prepared.

FERDINAND REVEALS HIS BIG IDEA

Ferdinand didn't look like much. He was short and still walked with a limp because of his war wounds.

But Ferdinand's big ideas soon made everyone forget about his size. Holding his globe by its handle, he began to talk about the unknown sea on the other side of the New World, which everyone called the South Sea.

He explained that Faleiro, his partner, had calculated that the South Sea was about 2,000 miles (3,200 kilometers) across . . . which meant that the Spice Islands were well within the Spanish half of the world, as laid down by the pope.

He told them that Faleiro had even managed to calculate **the exact location of a passage to the South Sea**.

Then Ferdinand read from his cousin Francisco's letters, conjuring pictures of idyllic tropical islands, repeating Serrão's words as if they were an invitation to the king himself.

Ferdinand beckoned, and a boy and a girl stepped before the king. It was Enrique, the slave Ferdinand had acquired in Malacca, and another slave, a girl from Indonesia.

Ferdinand told the court that his cousin was waiting for him in the Spice Islands, which sat on the edge of the South Sea. He showed them a globe on which the whole world was painted and traced the route across the Atlantic that he intended to take. He explained how he would cross to the New World, then sail south. Ferdinand pointed at the southern end of the globe and talked about the sea passage he believed would take them to the South Sea.

The court must have gasped. Now they understood:

⚙ Ferdinand was asking for funding to discover a strait that would lead Spain directly to the Spice Islands.

⚙ And it wouldn't mean going against their treaty with Portugal. The Spice Islands were well within the Spanish hemisphere—at least, that's what Ferdinand told them.

When the court historian asked what would happen if he didn't manage to find a strait, Ferdinand answered mysteriously that he *"would go the way taken by the Portuguese."* No one was quite sure what he meant.

Had Ferdinand swiped secret information from the Portuguese? Or was he just saying that because the Spaniards wanted Portugal's state secrets? Whatever the truth, **he had enchanted the court** and transported them to the blue skies and white sandy beaches of the Spice Islands.

By the time he left, the whole court was convinced that Ferdinand was the man to forge their route to the riches of the Spice Islands.

Success at Last!

A few weeks later, King Charles had good news for Ferdinand and Faleiro:

We order that the following contract with you be recorded:
Nobody else will be permitted to trade in spices at the Spice Islands for ten years.
You will be paid a twentieth part of all riches from the lands and islands that you discover.
You and your sons and heirs will henceforth have the titles of lieutenants and governors of the said lands.
You will be provided with five ships to be called the Armada de Molucca and you will receive a huge monthly salary.
You will both command the fleet and have full authority over your men.

King Charles had granted all of Ferdinand and Faleiro's demands. After his miserable life under King Manuel, **Ferdinand must have been astonished** and over the moon.

Yes, but I did wonder if it was all a bit too good to be true.

Too Good to Be True?

Unfortunately, it was. Charles had made Ferdinand and Faleiro very happy, but he'd left the moneymen in his court seething with rage. Instead of letting them invest and share in the treasure that Ferdinand was going to bring back from the Moluccas, **he'd decided to keep all the riches for himself**.

Now that they couldn't benefit from Ferdinand's expedition, the court was filled with envy. Suddenly, they questioned whether or not they could trust these Portuguese foreigners. Unfounded rumors started to spread about Ferdinand, and some courtiers demanded that a Spaniard should lead the expedition.

Charles had also trampled on powerful toes. The very influential archbishop Rodríguez de Fonseca usually made all the big decisions about which expeditions the king would sponsor. On the outside, Fonseca seemed polite and obedient, but inside, he was deeply suspicious of Ferdinand and Faleiro.

Most dangerous of all, the news of the expedition had reached Portugal, where Manuel had already ruined Ferdinand's name. There was a public outcry against him, and Manuel was now so filled with rage, he sent an ambassador, Álvaro da Costa, to bring Ferdinand back to Portugal.

When Ferdinand wouldn't budge, da Costa went to the Spanish king and told him a massive lie: Ferdinand and Faleiro had begged him to allow them to return to Portugal, he said. Would Charles give them permission to leave? Perhaps the voyage could be postponed.

Luckily, Charles saw through the lie and nothing came of da Costa's requests. But this wouldn't be the last time Manuel tried to stop Ferdinand. Portugal was Spain's rival and the angrier and more desperate Manuel became, the more Charles respected Ferdinand. Though his courtiers hated the Portuguese explorer, **the king didn't waver in his faith**.

6 FERDINAND SETS SAIL

Ferdinand had a ton of provisions to acquire, five ships to prepare and 235 men to recruit, but so many men wanted to come that he ended up with many more.

WHO'S WHO ONBOARD SHIP

The men Ferdinand recruited were from many different countries and **spoke a variety of languages**. Ordinary sailors were called mariners, carpenters kept the ship in good repair, gunners loaded and operated the guns . . .

Some of the roles onboard were more surprising . . .

It's four o'clock in the morning!

Priest

We pray every day.

Trumpeter—encouraged men to fight

Cabin boy—turned the hourglass and called out the time every half hour

Supplies

- 2,138 quintals* (two years' supply) of hardtack or ship's biscuit—a kind of bread that doesn't go moldy at sea.
- Seven cows to provide milk, then meat
- Three pigs
- Barrels of cheese
- Wine from Jerez
- Quince jam—for officers only
- Spare anchors, masts, sails, planks, ribs
- Tools—pincers, saws, awls, spades, hammers, nails, pickaxes
- Other tools—fish hooks, harpoons, nets
- Weapons—pikes, cannons, cannonballs
- Navigation—compasses, hourglasses, astrolabes, quadrants
- Drums and tambourines for entertainment
- Candles and lanterns
- Parchment to draw new maps, plus dried skins to make new parchment

Yum!

HARDTACK

Important to the story!

ASTROLABE

AWL

But nothing was ever easy for me, so of course there were problems from the start.

* one quintal = 100lb/45kg

FAREWELL TO FALEIRO

Before they were due to leave, Ferdinand's partner, Faleiro, began to behave strangely. He had always had a bad temper, but it was getting worse. He virtually stopped sleeping and was said to wander around "almost out of his mind."

Clearly, Faleiro was in no state to take up his role as captain of the *San Antonio*—the largest ship of the armada. King Charles issued a decree asking Faleiro to stay behind to prepare another armada. Ferdinand must have been relieved. **But who was going to take Faleiro's place?**

Now the scheming archbishop Fonseca seized his chance to step in. He appointed Juan de Cartagena, a man who had no experience at sea whatsoever—but did happen to be Fonseca's illegitimate son!

Fonseca also appointed two of his own close friends to captain two of the other ships. So now there were *three* Spanish captains and *two* Portuguese. Ferdinand would definitely have felt the Spaniards' intense dislike for him, but worse than that, with three against two, **the Spanish captains could overrule Ferdinand** at every turn!

Uh-oh!

THE ARMADA DE MOLUCCA

Ferdinand's ships:

- Were all black, with every surface painted with tar.

- Needed to be small and light enough to travel down the narrow Guadalquivir River that led from Seville to the Atlantic.

- Were the height of sixteenth-century technology.

Big and stable on the high seas

Trinidad, the flagship (100 tons, crew of 55, carrack)

The ships all took on far more men than they were allowed to carry

Biggest ship, useful for filling with spices

Big enough to fill with treasure

Commanded by Ferdinand

San Antonio
(120 tons, crew of 60, carrack)

Commanded by Juan de Cartagena (Fonseca's son—not to be trusted)

Concepción
(90 tons, crew of 45, carrack)

Commanded by Gaspar de Quesada (Spanish, hates Ferdinand)

Santiago
(75 tons, crew of 32, caravel)

Commanded by João Serrão (Portuguese)

Victoria
(85 tons, crew of 43, carrack)

Commanded by Luis de Mendosa (Spanish)

Fast and nimble, useful for racing ahead to check routes

Not the most important ship . . . yet!

Spies and Rabble-Rousers

Meanwhile, King Manuel had sent a spy, Sebastián Álvares, to make trouble for Ferdinand in Seville. **There were also rumors that Manuel had sent assassins!** King Charles was so worried that he assigned bodyguards to Ferdinand and Faleiro.

Álvares watched Ferdinand closely, looking for ways to sabotage his supplies.

One day, the usual crowd on the pier began to howl and point, claiming that Ferdinand was flying the Portuguese flag. (In fact, it was Ferdinand's own coat of arms, but that didn't matter to the mob.)

Things got worse when a town official called on people to seize Ferdinand. Another official argued against it and the two drew swords. In the scuffle, **one of Ferdinand's pilots was stabbed**.

Had Álvares stirred up the mob? He certainly reported the events back to King Manuel, who loved any negative news about Ferdinand.

Afterward, Ferdinand complained to King Charles, and the offenders were put in jail.

FERDINAND'S BIGGEST FAN

After all the trouble he'd had, Ferdinand must have been a bit taken aback when a young Venetian diplomat named Antonio Pigafetta came up to him on the docks, saying:

I'm your biggest fan!

That would have sounded a bit suspicious. Perhaps the man was a spy, sent by the scheming Fonseca! Who was he truly loyal to? Well, to Ferdinand's surprise, it quickly became very obvious that Pigafetta *was* a fan, through and through. **He absolutely idolized the captain.**

Pigafetta begged Ferdinand to take him along on the journey. He didn't want payment. He'd do all the lowly jobs and travel as a sobrasaliente—just like Ferdinand had when he'd set off on his first voyage.

Pigafetta said it wasn't riches he was looking for, but glory. He was also a fan of the Venetian explorer Marco Polo, who had written about his travels to China and back over 250 years earlier. The book had become a bestseller. Pigafetta dreamed of doing the same.

Ferdinand signed him up to write an account of the voyage, and thank goodness he did: **It's because of Pigafetta's diary that we know so many details.**

Pigafetta faithfully jotted down everything he saw, including the toxic atmosphere that surrounded Ferdinand. He wrote: *"The masters and the captains of the other ships of his company loved him not."*

Weighing Anchor at Last

Ferdinand's Armada of the Moluccas finally left Seville on August 10, 1519, two years after he'd arrived in Spain.

Ferdinand, aware that nobody trusted or liked him, was careful not to share his plans with the crew. Oh, they knew they were going to the Spice Islands, but they had no idea *how* they were going to get there. If the crew and officers didn't trust him, well, Ferdinand wasn't about to trust them either.

They docked at the Canary Islands to pick up more provisions for the long voyage ahead. While they were there, Ferdinand received two disturbing messages. One was a warning that two Portuguese fleets were on their way to arrest him. King Manuel was at it again! The other was from his father-in-law, Diogo Barbosa, warning that the Spanish captains were plotting a mutiny—led by Cartagena!

Ferdinand told no one about the warnings. Instead, he ordered his ships to set sail before the extra provisions had been carried aboard.

To evade King Manuel's ships, Ferdinand led the armada south, down the coast of Africa, instead of sailing west across the Atlantic as planned. Cartagena complained bitterly and demanded an explanation, but Ferdinand just reminded his captains that they had sworn to follow him.

The change of direction must have thrown King Manuel's ships. But the armada ran into several weeks of horrible weather. The sea rose in gnashing waves that tossed the ships about as if they were toys. **Sharks began to circle them**, hoping a sailor would be tossed overboard.

Just as the men were despairing, dazzling green haloes of light appeared on the yardarm of the *Trinidad*, Ferdinand's ship. The sailors fell to their knees, weeping, convinced that it was a sign from God, and they were all about to die.

But what they had seen was a natural weather phenomenon called St. Elmo's Fire. It's caused by electrical charges generated during thunderstorms. But the sailors didn't know that. After the fires died down, they assumed God must be telling them that Ferdinand was a very important man.

MUTINY

St. Elmo's Fire didn't stop the Spanish captains confronting Ferdinand about their strange route, though. They suspected that Ferdinand was actually working with King Manuel. Cartagena even **blamed Ferdinand for the storms**!

One day, Cartagena, backed by the two other Spanish captains, confronted Ferdinand. But when Cartagena gave the signal to attack, Ferdinand's men rushed into the room with drawn swords.

Ferdinand's men dragged Cartagena up on deck and put him in the stocks. It was a humiliating sight for the other officers. This sort of punishment was usually reserved for lowly sailors. And for a Portuguese man to do this to a Spaniard! It was shocking.

The two other Spanish captains begged Ferdinand to spare Cartagena, promising that they themselves would keep him under lock and key.

It was a tricky moment. Cartagena was the son of Archbishop Fonseca, **one of the most powerful men in Spain**. Ferdinand must have struggled with wanting to make an example of him and worrying about the consequences when the archbishop found out what had happened.

In the end, Ferdinand agreed to let the two Spanish captains keep charge of Cartagena and gave command of Cartagena's ship to another man.

THE NEW WORLD

It was November, three months after they'd left Spain, and the armada was finally sailing west, across the Atlantic. But life onboard was no bed of roses.

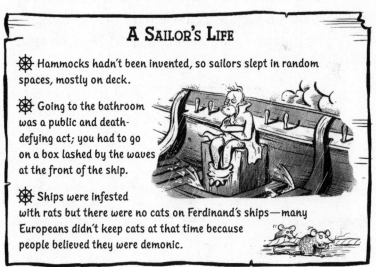

A SAILOR'S LIFE

⚙ Hammocks hadn't been invented, so sailors slept in random spaces, mostly on deck.

⚙ Going to the bathroom was a public and death-defying act; you had to go on a box lashed by the waves at the front of the ship.

⚙ Ships were infested with rats but there were no cats on Ferdinand's ships—many Europeans didn't keep cats at that time because people believed they were demonic.

- ⚙ The men cooked for themselves and ate from wooden plates with knives that they carried with them.

- ⚙ They mostly ate porridge, bread, or hardtack biscuits, which lasted for years! There was meat and wine on Sundays, Tuesdays, and Thursdays.

- ⚙ They bathed and washed their clothes in seawater.

- ⚙ Ships often carried a few street children to do the dirty jobs onboard, but only rich kids served as cabin boys. Officers brought their own pages and lived in better conditions than the crew.

They completed the ocean crossing and docked at a natural harbor in Brazil.

The men were nervous. The Portuguese had staked a claim to Brazil. And many knew that the explorer Amerigo Vespucci had described **a gruesome culture of cannibalism** among the local Guaraní tribespeople.

But Ferdinand wasn't afraid. He quickly got on with laying his own claim to the area.

I, Ferdinand Magellan, name this bay Bahia Santa Lucía!

Actually, we call it something else . . . but don't mind us!

The men shouldn't have worried. As the ships entered the harbor, the locals swam out to meet them, welcoming them warmly. They traded fresh food, geese, and chickens for tiny Spanish trinkets. Pigafetta even managed to buy **five chickens with one playing card**! The Guaraní also valued other metals over gold and enthusiastically traded gold and food for nails, hammers, hooks, and mirrors.

One of the crew members fell in love with a woman and tried to run away with her. He had to be arrested and spent the rest of the stop confined to his ship.

When the crew celebrated Mass on the shore, the Guaraní joined them. Pigafetta reckoned they would be easily converted to Christianity. But later Ferdinand learned that the locals had been welcoming because they believed that the fleet's arrival had magically brought the rain.

BLACK GEESE AND SEA WOLVES

The armada finally left Brazil on December 27, 1519. They were in the southern hemisphere, so the seasons were all topsy-turvy. It was winter in Europe, but summer in Brazil, and Ferdinand hoped to find the channel before winter came.

But **Faleiro's charts were wrong**. The coast rolled on and on and on, and the weather got colder and colder. The jungles gave way to icy wastelands, populated by strange, large birds that couldn't fly. Pigafetta described them in his diary as "black geese." They were actually penguins.

Pigafetta described another strange creature, like a calf, with small round ears, but with feet attached to its body that looked like human hands. He called it a "sea wolf" because it lived in the water and swam like a fish—today we'd say they were sea lions.

Twice, sailors hunting the sea wolves on the shore were stranded by sudden storms.

Even though there was plenty of meat (especially sea wolf and black goose) and fish, Ferdinand decided to reduce food rations. He must have been nervous, not knowing how long they might be at sea.

By now, Ferdinand had told the crew that they were looking for a strait, but the men couldn't believe such a sea passage existed, and they started getting restless and angry. They thought Ferdinand was leading them into danger. Surely, they argued, King Charles didn't want them to die?

But Ferdinand would not be moved. The more they suffered, he told them, the greater their reward.

By March, the fleet found itself in an icy wasteland on the coast of the country we now call Argentina. They stopped here in a sheltered bay to rest and repair the ships. Ferdinand named it Puerto San Julián (or Port St. Julian).

On Easter Sunday, April 1, Cartagena—who was supposed to be in chains—led a group of thirty armed men onto the ship he used to command, the *San Antonio*. With him was Quesada, one of the Spanish captains who had promised to control Cartagena, as well as another Spaniard, Juan Sebastián Elcano, from the *Concepción*.

The crew of the *San Antonio* resisted, but after the mutineers killed a crew member and arrested the Portuguese captain who had replaced Cartagena, the ship's men felt **they had no choice but to give in**. To win over the crew, the mutineers opened up the food stores and **invited them to eat**. It worked! And soon two more ships joined the mutiny: the *Victoria* and the *Concepción*.

Cartagena now commanded three of the five ships!

7   FERDINAND FINDS THE WAY

So why did they mutiny?

Life onboard ship was no picnic. The ships leaked. The holds stank of salted fish and rotting food. Shipworms drilled through anything made of wood. The men couldn't keep clean—have you ever tried washing with salt water? Their heads were itching with lice, and their sleeping places were crawling with bedbugs and cockroaches! And the rats! Well, they did become useful later on . . . but that's getting ahead of the story.

So, living on the ship was bad enough, but imagine working for someone like Ferdinand.

I have such vision, courage, and determination . . .

He's bossy, argumentative, and _so_ stubborn.

Ferdinand saw himself not as his men's employer but as their master. **He pushed them to the limits** without thinking of giving them anything in return. He made them pray twice a day, and the boys who operated the hourglasses had to chant prayers loudly enough for the rest of the ship to hear.

He banned swearing, cards, and gambling (though the crew still played when he wasn't looking). He demanded that they call him "Captain General" at all times.

He ordered the other ships to approach his at sunset every day, to salute him.

He kept details of their mission secret until the last minute, even from the captains of the other ships. Life was hard enough onboard without not knowing where you were going, how long it would take, or when you were going to go home again. **The men felt frightened and unsafe.**

Most of all, there was a lack of trust. The Spanish didn't trust Ferdinand because he was Portuguese. The sailors didn't trust him because he seemed willing to sacrifice their lives to get what he wanted.

A WHIFF OF SUSPICION

Ferdinand had heard whispers of a second mutiny. So, as the mutineers were finalizing their plan, Ferdinand was furiously readying his ship, the *Trinidad*, for attack. He also got lucky: Even before the mutineers seized the *San Antonio*, one of their longboats that had been taking messages from one mutinous ship to another had drifted on a strong current right into Ferdinand's ship.

Ferdinand welcomed the men aboard and shrewdly offered them a lavish feast and plenty of wine. After weeks of hunger, they couldn't resist! They gorged on food and probably drank too much, because it wasn't long before they were chatting away to Ferdinand about **Cartagena's plan to capture and kill him**.

It was valuable information for Ferdinand, and it set his mind whirring.

FERDINAND'S CUNNING PLAN

After they seized the *San Antonio*, the leaders of the mutiny sent a list of demands.

The list enraged Ferdinand. He felt like they were close to a breakthrough! How could they quit now? But he was ready to deal with them.

Surrender!
TURN BACK!
GIVE US MORE
FOOD!
GIVE US MORE
~~FOOD~~ WINE!

He agreed to discuss the mutineers' terms onboard one of their ships, but instead of heading for the *San Antonio*, Ferdinand sent a boat full of men to the *Victoria*.

Now that the *Victoria* was under control, he had to deal with the *San Antonio* and the *Concepción*. Ferdinand's three ships (*Trinidad*, *Santiago*, and *Victoria*) changed position to block the mouth of the bay. The *Concepción* and the *San Antonio*, positioned deeper in the harbor, couldn't escape, but they were too far away for cannon fire to reach them.

The mutineers were still refusing to surrender, so that night, one of Magellan's men sneaked onboard the *Concepción* and cut the cable connecting the ship to its anchor. The crew of the *Concepción* woke up the next morning to find their ship had **drifted right up to the *Trinidad***.

Ferdinand opened fire and his men threw grappling hooks to draw the *Concepción* closer. Once

Ferdinand's men were aboard, the mutineers didn't have much trouble switching their allegiance back to Ferdinand.

Most of the leaders of the mutiny met very unpleasant ends: tortured, chopped to pieces, and their body parts left as a warning on the beach at St. Julian.

All forty of the men who joined the mutiny were condemned to death, though when Ferdinand realized he wouldn't have enough crew to sail the ships, he promptly changed the sentence to hard labor!

But when two men tried to stage yet another mutiny, Ferdinand couldn't bring himself to execute them. One was a priest, and Ferdinand was too religious to kill a man of God (though not too religious to chop up the other ringleaders). The other was Cartagena. How could he execute the son of one of the most powerful men in Spain?

Ferdinand's solution? He put the two men ashore in the barren, icy wilderness of St. Julian . . . and **sailed off without them**.

HERE BE A SHIPWRECK!

In May 1520, the armada had been sailing for nine months. As they pushed farther south, the weather turned grimmer and grimmer. They had now sailed off the edges of their map and reached "Here Be Dragons" territory.

Ferdinand decided to shelter in Port St. Julian until the worst of the weather was over. He had the men empty the ships to give them a thorough cleaning, washing down the wood with vinegar. When they began to reload their provisions, Ferdinand discovered that his suppliers had cheated him . . . **they only had a third of the provisions they needed**.

After the mutiny, Ferdinand had been more generous with food. But now he cut rations again.

Luckily, the "black geese" and the "sea wolves" were still plentiful.

To save time, he decided to send the little caravel, the *Santiago*, ahead to search for the strait while they finished cleaning and repairing the bigger ships.

But seventy miles away from the rest of the fleet, a storm blew up and the *Santiago* was wrecked. The thirty-seven men onboard barely managed to wade through the frozen waters to the rocky shore. They watched as their ship broke up in front of them and its wreckage and **all their provisions were carried away by the sea**.

Uh-oh!

The castaways had to trek for miles over mountains. They reached a three-mile-wide river, built a raft, and sent two men across to get help. It took them eleven days to walk back to the fleet, in freezing weather, with barely any food. When they arrived, they were so wasted and skeletal that Ferdinand hardly recognized them.

Once the men had told their story, a team of twenty-four men set off on foot to rescue the rest of the *Santiago*'s crew. The rescuers took four days to reach the stranded men, who had managed to survive on shellfish and what local vegetation they could eat. They ferried the survivors across the river two or three at a time on their tiny, makeshift raft.

This time, it took them a week to trudge their way back to the fleet, but miraculously the thirty-seven-man crew of the *Santiago* and the men who'd been sent to rescue them all survived! Ferdinand was so relieved that **he was actually generous** with the food and wine for a change.

Land of the Giants

One day, after two months in the icy wilderness, Ferdinand heard a strange sound. Looking through his spyglass, he saw a huge man on the beach, singing and dancing, and every so often scooping up sand to throw on his bald head.

Pigafetta wrote in his diary: *"He had a very large face, painted round with red, and his eyes also were painted round with yellow, and in the middle of his cheeks, he had two hearts painted."* The giant was wearing enormous boots.

The men begged Ferdinand to sail away,

remembering those stories of man-eating tribes. But Ferdinand went ashore, ordering one of his men to befriend the giant. "Dance and sing, if you have to," Ferdinand told the sailor.

The man crept slowly toward the giant. And when the giant spotted him, the sailor began to dance, as Ferdinand had ordered. Everyone watching held their breath. **Was the giant going to kill him and eat him?**

The two men danced together, then the sailor led the giant to Ferdinand.

At the sight of the crewmen, the giant became afraid, pointing up at the sky. Pigafetta wrote that maybe he believed they'd come from Heaven.

It's probable the giants were ancestors of modern-day Tehuelche people, but of course, Ferdinand gave them a new name. He called them Patagonians—it's said the name came from *Pata de Cano*, which was rumored to mean "people with big feet"—because of their huge furry boots. The name stuck, and the region is still called Patagonia today.

But were they really giants? Pigafetta was probably exaggerating. Today's Tehuelche are tall, averaging six feet (1.8 m). In medieval times, the average European was just five feet six inches (1.67 m), so the men might have seemed huge, but they weren't actual giants.

It was winter now, and while the armada waited for the bad weather to pass, the crew spent their time befriending the Patagonians, learning about their customs, and hunting guanacos—llama-like animals the Patagonians ate and turned into furry boots.

Then Ferdinand had an idea. When Columbus had arrived in Lisbon all those years ago, he'd kidnapped two natives from one of the islands that he'd discovered to show off when he got back. Ferdinand dreamed of doing the same.

He invited several Patagonians onboard ship and

presented them with gifts of knives, scissors, mirrors, bells, and glass. The giants were fascinated. When Ferdinand had iron shackles put on the ankles of two of the Patagonians, they thought those were gifts too. But **they soon realized that they were prisoners**.

Ferdinand put the two shackled Patagonians on the *Trinidad* and the *Victoria* and had the rest of them escorted back to shore. The rest of the Patagonians were so upset that they ran away . . . and later the Europeans were ambushed in a hail of poisoned arrows that killed one crew member.

After that, the armada hurried on its way with the kidnapped Patagonians onboard. Pigafetta spent many hours with them, getting to know them and even learning some of their language.

Tragically the two Patagonians died during the journey, but ninety years later Pigafetta's account about them inspired William Shakespeare to write *The Tempest*, a play about shipwreck survivors who wash up on an island where they meet a wild man and other strange characters.

SEEKING THE STRAIT

Ferdinand probably didn't have any secret information about a strait, as his captains suspected, but at this point **turning back just wasn't an option**.

The fleet crept down the coastline, turning into any opening they found, only to turn back again when the inlets brought them to rivers or bays or freshwater channels that clearly wouldn't lead to an ocean.

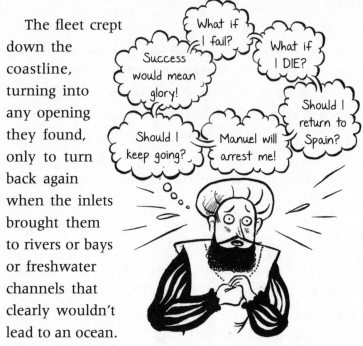

On October 21, 1520, ten months after they had left Brazil and six months after they left Patagonia, Ferdinand spotted a cape (a rocky point sticking out of the mainland into the open sea). It marked a wide opening from the sea, leading to the west, and **its beach was covered with whale skeletons**. Could this be a migration route whales used to get from one ocean to the other?

The opening led them to a narrow passage with deep salt water and strong currents.

The men shouted in excitement.

They had found it at last. Ferdinand's strait.

Cape Virgenes—Named after Saint Ursula because they arrived there on her feast day. She traveled everywhere with 11,000 virgins.

Port St. Julian—Ferdinand punished the mutineers and met the Patagonians here.

Tierra del Fuego—Ferdinand thought he saw fires on the shore here.

OUT

IN

STRAIT OF MAGELLAN

THE STRAIT WAS NOT STRAIGHT

Ferdinand's captains weren't quite so excited. They were about to plunge deeper into the unknown. If they *hadn't* found the strait, they could have been on their way home by now. They only had three months of food supplies left and even if they survived, they had no idea how long it would take to get to the Spice Islands.

Not only that, **the strait looked terrifying**. The ice on the shore seemed to wriggle and there were unstable cracking glaciers everywhere.

Through a thick mist, they could see distant fires and plumes of smoke. Ferdinand named the place

Tierra del Fuego—Land of Fire. But the men didn't dare go ashore. What if the fires were set by dangerous locals? (In fact, they weren't man-made at all—they were probably caused by lightning.)

It also turned out that Ferdinand's strait was not one neat, straight sea highway to the other side of the New World, as he might have imagined. It was a series of confusing channels meandering between high cliffs. How were they supposed to know which channel to follow?

By this time, it was midsummer in the southern hemisphere. The days were long, and the nights were short—**three hours, to be exact**. There were longer hours of light so the fleet could make up for lost time, but the weather was still stormy. Ferdinand had to be careful. He couldn't afford to lose another ship.

He sent the *San Antonio* and the *Concepción* ahead to figure out which way they should go. The scouting missions were dangerous, and more than once, the ships lost their way and were very nearly wrecked.

FERDINAND EXPLAINS: HOW TO NAVIGATE A STRAIT

I had to guide the armada through hundreds of miles of unknown territory!

We didn't know what lay ahead, so I had men perched high up on the masts to look out for barriers and dangers!

I feel sick!

So that we didn't follow an inland channel by mistake, I had the men taste the water to make sure it was always salty.

Hmm . . . I'm getting a strong salty note and . . . is that a faint undercurrent of whale poop?

I sent longboats out ahead to check if the way was safe.

I don't feel safe.

I want my mommy!

Yet Another Mutiny

There was a skilled pilot on the *San Antonio* named Estêvão Gomes. He was Portuguese, but he didn't get along with Ferdinand at all. In fact, according to Pigafetta's diary, he *hated* Ferdinand. Gomes tried to persuade Ferdinand to turn back, but Ferdinand just ignored him.

So Gomes decided **he didn't need Ferdinand's permission**. He just went ahead and did it. With other mutineers, he attacked the *San Antonio*'s captain, who was loyal to Ferdinand, stabbing him in the leg. Then the mutineers shackled him and turned the ship toward Spain.

Meanwhile, when the *San Antonio* failed to return from its scouting mission, Ferdinand sent his ships up and down the strait to search for it. He even ordered one ship to sail all the way back to the entrance of the strait.

When they couldn't find the *San Antonio*, Ferdinand planted a cross on one of the small islands with a pot buried underneath it. Inside was a message with details of the course they were going to take, just in case the men of the *San Antonio* returned to find it.

It was obvious to everyone, though, that the worst had happened—**the *San Antonio* had turned back and was heading home.** It was yet another mutiny and a massive disaster: The *San Antonio* was the largest ship in the armada and it carried most of the fleet's food supplies.

Mutiny was a crime, but the mutineers thought they could get away with it. Once they told the king what Ferdinand had done to Cartagena and the others, they reasoned, surely he would realize what a tyrant Ferdinand had become and pardon them. One thing was for sure: They were going to do everything they could to blacken Ferdinand's name.

But while he was waiting for the *San Antonio*, **Ferdinand received incredible news.** While returning from another scouting mission, the *Victoria*'s crew had seen a cape, and beyond the cape, another ocean.

8   FERDINAND CROSSES AN OCEAN

At last, here it was, the ocean that explorers had been glimpsing from the hills of the New World since 1513—the very same ocean that Ferdinand believed his cousin Francisco could see from the Spice Islands.

Ferdinand named it the Pacific Ocean, because it seemed so still and calm. It was a wish as much as anything. Ferdinand and his crew had endured more than a year of hunger, thirst, and misery. Roughly 260 crew had sailed out from Seville and **almost a quarter had died**. Only three of the armada's five ships remained. After the turbulence of the strait, Ferdinand was hoping that the Spice Islands would be just a few days' sailing away.

How was he supposed to know that the Pacific Ocean is one-and-a-half times the size of the Atlantic and bigger than all dry land on Earth put together?

HUNGRY

The water remained smooth as the climate warmed. December passed.

The year 1520 became 1521. January. February.
Hope turned into boredom.
Boredom turned into fear.
And still they sailed on.

Provisions were running out. The seal meat they had hunted and preserved with salt was now rotting. The hardtack biscuits had crumbled to powder. **Everything was swarming with maggots.** Their drinking water had turned yellow. The stores smelled of rat pee.

The men were so hungry that they began to scrape off the oxhide that was wrapped around the masts to keep them dry.

Some men ate sawdust, and other men bought rats from enterprising rat-catchers. But soon, even the supply of rats was used up.

First we soak the hides in seawater, then we roast them on the fire.

Sick

And then the men began to fall ill. Their gums puffed up. Old wounds opened up again. Broken bones that had already set broke again. Legs swelled. Painful spots and boils began to sprout all over their bodies.

Scurvy had arrived.

FERDINAND EXPLAINS: THE SCOURGE OF SCURVY

We Europeans had never seen scurvy before we went on long sea voyages, but during the Age of Exploration, the disease sometimes killed half a ship's crew.

Scurvy is caused by a lack of vitamin C and basically stops the body from producing the tissue that holds it together.

Symptoms include:

What's happening to me?

teeth falling out

odor

sunken eyes

Help! Zombie!

wounds reopening

boils

pale skin

no energy

pain

Scurvy struck on long ocean journeys when sailors had no fresh food.

There was a cure—fresh fruit—but it was discovered and forgotten over the years.

Of Vasco da Gama's crew of 160, 100 men died of scurvy. Arab sailors healed the rest with oranges. But da Gama still believed in another cure:

Men should wash their mouths out with their own pee!

D'oh!

← Vasco da Gama

In 1795, the British Royal Navy finally realized the disease was caused by a lack of vitamin C and ordered a daily dose of lemon or lime juice for all sailors.

The crew on Ferdinand's ships believed that scurvy was caused by the foul air belowdecks. Ferdinand urged everyone to sleep on deck. But nothing seemed to work, and **the sick had no choice but to keep working**, even as their teeth began to fall out.

Ferdinand surprised everyone by personally looking after the sick. Perhaps he was a softy after all. Or maybe he just needed the men to get well enough to sail the ship.

Oh, Captain, you're not so evil after all!

It's Captain GENERAL to you, idiot!

Ferdinand couldn't understand why none of the high-ranking officers fell ill. It was only hundreds of years later that historians realized the officers were spared because their rations included quince jam, which gave them some essential vitamin C.

Scores of ordinary sailors were stricken, and men began dying. All Ferdinand could do was have their bodies wrapped in sheets, weighed down with cannonballs, and **dropped overboard**.

STARSTRUCK

Lying on deck one night, staring up at the sky, Pigafetta noticed the stars bunching up in two puffs.

Oooh . . . pretty!

Several small stars clustered together are seen, which have the appearance of two clouds of mist.

He was just doing his usual obsessive diary keeping—but it turned out **he'd made an important astronomical observation**.

The star clusters were, in fact, two dwarf galaxies orbiting the Milky Way (the galaxy that contains our solar system). For a long time, these galaxies were believed to be the nearest to Earth. They came to be known as the Magellanic Clouds.

But, of course, other people had spotted them before:

The Pacific Ocean remained peaceful. But there was just too much of it.

Sharks began circling the ships, as if they were sniffing out their next meal.

Even Ferdinand began to despair. When he realized his calculations were all wrong, **he threw his maps overboard**, crying, *"The Moluccas are not to be found in their appointed place!'*

Even the normally chirpy Pigafetta began to lose hope. *"I believe that nevermore will any man undertake to make such a voyage,"* he wrote.

There was no land in sight, and the Pacific Ocean seemed to have no end. In fact, **there are 25,000 islands in the Pacific Ocean**. But somehow, the Armada of the Moluccas failed to spot a single one until . . .

LAND AT LAST!

Early one morning, a whopping 98 days after they had entered the Pacific, the watchman high up in the crow's nest screamed, "Tierra! Tierra!" which is Spanish for "Land! Land!"

Ferdinand was so excited he climbed halfway up the mast to see for himself.

It was true. They could see shadows standing out against the sheen of the ocean, and those shadows turned out to be two islands.

They may have been weak, but the men could have danced with relief.

Even so, Ferdinand couldn't help feeling a tiny bit disappointed. His cousin, Francisco, had described the islands as being like a string of emeralds, some of which were volcanoes rising out of the sea.

But it's not the Spice Islands.

As they approached, dozens of tiny sailing boats came speeding toward them from the shore. The men had never seen such cool little sea vessels. *"They were going so fast, they seemed to fly,"* one crew member wrote in his log. The locals called the boats "proas."

Sails: palm leaves sewn together

Both ends the same shape, so sailor turns the boat, not the sail, to change direction

This side flat

Speeds up to 20 knots (23 mph/37 km/h)

The outrigger stops the boat capsizing

Oars for steering

This side rounded

Cool!

The boats circled the fleet, boldly bumping right up against the ships.

Tall men with shaved heads climbed up onto the deck until it was packed. The islanders—who later came to be called Chamorros—seemed friendly enough . . . but then they began to help themselves to everything they could take from the decks.

Alarmed, the crew tried to stop them. A scuffle broke out. The islanders fought with sticks as the crewmen hurried to defend themselves.

Then another group of Chamorros turned up. They climbed onto the ships carrying bundles and began to hand them out. It was food! The starved crewmen stopped fighting and began to eat. When they finished, the Chamorros began to fight them again!

But since **they were suddenly very outnumbered**, Ferdinand commanded his men to stop fighting. Good call! The Chamorros stopped fighting too. They took more food out of their boats and handed it around.

Soon Ferdinand's men found themselves trading glass beads for coconut and fish.

But when the Chamorros finally left the ships, Ferdinand discovered that they had taken one of his small boats.

The Chamorros had had no idea that people existed outside of their islands. They didn't understand the European idea of owning things. They gave their stuff freely . . . so they thought they could take other people's stuff just as freely.

But Ferdinand hadn't figured this out. His boat was worth more to him than the friendship of these strangers. With forty of his men, Ferdinand went ashore and attacked the Chamorros, burning their houses and killing several of their people.

Later Pigafetta described how the Chamorros, who were armed with spears tipped with fish bones—for catching flying fish, not for fighting—**had never seen bows and arrows before**. Pigafetta watched them pull the arrows out of their bodies with surprise before they died.

While the Chamorros fled and hid in the jungle, Ferdinand and his men looted their homes, taking pigs, chickens, fish, fruit, and fresh water. When Ferdinand finally ordered his fleet to sail away, the Chamorros chased them in their proas, throwing stones. On the shore, the women wept for their dead.

BACK FROM THE DEAD

Ferdinand sailed due west, hoping that his next stop would be the Spice Islands. In fact, the Spice Islands were just off to the southwest.

But at least **everyone was in a much more hopeful mood** now that they'd restocked the hold with fresh food and water. Ferdinand's heart must have leaped when the lookout screamed "Tierra!" once more, even though the land he'd spotted still looked nothing like the Spice Islands.

It was March 16, 1521, one year and six grueling months since they'd left Spain.

European explorers had mapped parts of China, Japan, Vietnam, Laos, Cambodia, Malaysia, and Indonesia . . . but these islands did not appear anywhere. The armada had landed in the previously uncharted islands now known as the Philippines.

The first island they came across is known as Samar today. Ferdinand stared at its shore, all jungly, with palm trees and waterfalls tumbling off cliffs. **It looked like paradise.**

But the ships couldn't anchor safely, so they moved on to an island called Homonhon, where the shore was lined with strange palm trees that had long, thin trunks and hard fruit as big as a man's head.

Ferdinand ordered his men to pitch tents on the shore.

I hereby name these islands after Lazarus, who was raised from the dead!

Landing here saved them from death. Then 22 years later, they named our islands the Philippines, after *their* Spanish king, Philip II.

MEETING THE NEIGHBORS

One day, a large boat loaded with nine men approached. Ferdinand barked at the crew to have their weapons at the ready, but just in case they turned out to be friendly, he also quickly pulled out goods to trade—cheap trinkets like bells, scissors, red caps, colored hankerchiefs, satins, wool, robes from Turkey, and mirrors.

The strangers were elaborately dressed and friendly. They communicated with Ferdinand by acting out what they wanted to say as if they were playing a game of charades.

Ferdinand promptly offered them his gifts. In return, they offered him a jar of palm wine, fish, coconuts, and . . . bananas.

The men had never seen a banana before.

Seeing the sick sailors, the strangers taught Ferdinand how to separate the milk and flesh from a coconut. **It was literally a lifesaver!** Over the next few days, the men began to recover—though they still blamed bad air for the scurvy.

Ferdinand invited his new friends onto one of the ships and showed them samples of the spices he wanted. He must have watched carefully as the islanders examined them. Did they know what they were? And, if so, would they be able to direct him to the Spice Islands?

To his delight, the islanders did recognize the spices and said they grew on the nearby islands! Ferdinand was so happy that he ordered his gunners to fire their rifles in honor of the guests. But **the explosions terrified the islanders**, and several of them tried to leap off the boat and into the sea.

Ferdinand quickly calmed them down and persuaded them not to jump. But in establishing that the islanders hadn't seen weapons like his before, Ferdinand might have felt a sneaking sense of power.

At that moment, he must have remembered his contract with King Charles. His mission was not just to find a sea route to the Far East, but to conquer lands and claim them for the throne. And **here were people who he could conquer.** Had his luck changed at last?

They were generous and easily frightened—it looked like things were finally going my way!

9   FERDINAND THE CONQUEROR

Remember Enrique? The slave Ferdinand acquired in Malacca? Well, he'd been at Ferdinand's side the whole voyage. So far, little had been recorded about him. Pigafetta only began to write about him when they got to the Philippines. Ferdinand's own diaries have never been found, but there is one surviving document that does feature Enrique: Ferdinand's will.

In the will, Ferdinand wanted to leave 600,000 maravedis to his wife and two young sons—a fortune! He also left 30,000 maravedis to his illegitimate son (yes, he had one and he was actually also on the voyage); and 10,000 maravedis to Enrique, which was a generous sum, considering the way people treated slaves during Ferdinand's day. Ferdinand must have been fond of Enrique, because that was not his only gift to the slave: He also declared that upon his death, **Enrique would be set free!**

And that's a very important point to remember for this next part of the story.

A REALLY GOOD TALK

After a lovely rest at Homonhon, Ferdinand sailed on. One evening, they were nearing an island called

Limasawa, when a boat approached them. Ferdinand peered into the gloom and saw that the men in the boat were warriors. It probably made him a little bit nervous, but perhaps the memory of his kindly welcome in Homonhon—and the way **his guns had struck fear in the natives**—steadied his nerves.

They could hear the men speaking in low voices as the boat came closer. Enrique, who was standing beside Ferdinand on deck, suddenly called out in a foreign language. The men in the boat replied. Ferdinand couldn't believe it. Enrique was soon chatting away with the strangers in the same language.

Maayong gabii![1]

Makasulti ka ug binisaya?[2]

Whoa! You speak their language!

1. Good evening!
2. Can you speak Visayan?

Until that moment, Enrique had probably spoken to everyone on the ship in Portuguese. How did he know Visayan? There is one possibility.

Ferdinand had found Enrique in Malacca . . . but maybe he didn't come from there. Had Malaccan slave traders captured him from these islands?

For Ferdinand, the moment he realized that Enrique could speak to the warriors, **everything changed**.

When Rajah Kulambo, the local king, arrived, Ferdinand chatted easily with him through Enrique, trading presents and becoming friends. By the end of the following day, they had agreed to become blood brothers! It was a traditional custom there back then, called a blood compact, but it is *not* recommended today: The two men cut their chests, mixed the blood in a vessel of coconut wine—and drank it!

Then Ferdinand invited Rajah Kulambo onto his boat, and with Enrique's help told the story of his exciting voyage from the other side of the world. To give it a dramatic finish, Ferdinand ordered his gunner to fire a salute . . . and watched with satisfaction as **poor Kulambo nearly fell off his chair**, terrified.

After soothing Kulambo's nerves, Ferdinand ordered one of the crew to put on an armored breastplate, then he had three of his men strike him with swords and daggers, to show how it protected him.

Kulambo was silent.

Ferdinand smiled to himself. The king was smart. He got that **Ferdinand's demonstration was not an entertainment** but a show of force: a warning.

Then the Captain General just couldn't help himself. He asked the king if he thought that one of Ferdinand's armored men was worth one hundred of his own?

The king could only agree.

Island Kingdoms

Over the next few weeks, the flotilla sailed through the Philippine islands, meeting more of the rajahs who ruled over them.

Unlike the Chamorros, these islanders were used to meeting outsiders and trading with foreigners. In fact, "rajah" is a Sanskrit word that came all the way from India. They served their food on great porcelain plates purchased from Chinese sea merchants. They knew a lot about spices and had probably traveled to the Spice Islands. They loved gold, coconuts, and music . . .

FERDINAND EMPOWERED

As the days passed, Ferdinand became even more confident.

Ferdinand before the Philippines . . .   Ferdinand after the Philippines.

He was walking in the footsteps of the explorers he had admired as a boy—discovering other cultures, making allies, and winning territory—and he'd overcome incredible odds to get there. By finding the strait and crossing the Pacific Ocean, he knew **he had made history**.

On Easter Sunday, fifty men came onshore wearing their best clothes. The islanders watched as they knelt in front of a cross and celebrated the Catholic Mass. Afterward, they feasted with their new friends.

The islanders' warmth and kindness must have made Ferdinand feel quite protective toward them. It was almost as if the people had already declared him their viceroy . . . Eventually, he asked the king

whether he had any enemies. Kulambo named two island kings he didn't get along with, and Ferdinand, perhaps a bit drunk with power (and coconut wine), promised to return one day to defeat them as a gift.

Making Allies

The fleet sailed on, taking Rajah Kulambo with it. Perhaps Ferdinand realized it would be useful to have a local rajah along. The islanders would accept them more easily, and if things went badly . . . well, they could always turn Kulambo into a hostage.

They entered a channel between two islands, small Mactan and larger Cebu.

On Cebu, the shore was lined with houses, and the water was busy with proas. The people didn't seem particularly surprised to see the three black ships anchoring, but when Ferdinand ordered artillery to be fired, **they were terrified.** Ferdinand wanted the king of Cebu, Rajah Humabon, to see his power.

Spotting Kulambo, Humabon welcomed Ferdinand warmly. But then he demanded a present from Ferdinand. All visiting traders "paid tribute," he said. A ship from Siam (present-day Thailand) had, in fact, just left, having done exactly that.

Ferdinand was indignant. His king, he explained, was Charles of Spain, who was far more important than Humabon; it should be Humabon doing the gift giving! If the king wished for peace, he would have peace, Ferdinand blustered. But if he wished for war, then **Ferdinand could give him war**.

Ferdinand and Humabon glared at each other. But then one of the men in Humabon's court stepped forward and whispered in the king's ear. It was a trader from the Siamese ship who had stayed behind.

Whatever he said changed Humabon's attitude entirely.

Suddenly, Humabon turned into the hospitable host. He offered them refreshments: many jars of wine and meat on porcelain platters. As the Europeans feasted, Kulambo had a word with the king of Cebu.

The next day, Humabon offered a tribute to King Charles. Not only that, he too performed the blood compact with Ferdinand.

What did the Siamese trader say to change the king's mind? Pigafetta thought it was something like:

"Treat them well, it will be well for you, if you treat them ill, so much the worse it will be for you." News of Portugal devastating parts of India, Malacca, and the Indian Ocean had probably reached Cebu.

After the blood compact, Ferdinand ordered another demonstration of armor. The sight of an armored seaman withstanding blows from swords and daggers had the desired effect—**Humabon was very disturbed.**

Religion

Perhaps it was all that coconut wine the rajahs kept plying him with. Perhaps it was because he felt safe. Or perhaps it was because he felt like he had the power to change things. Ferdinand's thoughts turned to religion.

With Enrique to translate for him, Ferdinand began to talk to his hosts about the Bible.

His audience reacted enthusiastically. They asked many questions and even **begged Ferdinand to leave a priest with them** so that they could learn more about his faith.

How did Ferdinand feel to hear these rajahs so moved by his preaching? After the long, hard months he'd spent fighting to be accepted—by King Manuel, by the Spanish, by his own men—here were people with open hearts. Ferdinand wept with joy.

He ordered his chaplain, Father Valderrama, to baptize the islanders.

Of course, the islanders already had their own belief system. Everywhere on the island—on the beaches and in people's houses— were carved spirit figures that Ferdinand referred to as their "idols."

Ferdinand told the islanders that if they were going to be baptized, they would have to **burn all their spirit figures**.

Over the next few days there wa a lively atmosphere on the island as the priest carried out baptism after baptism. Humabon, his queen, and more than two thousand of his people were christened.

Even the trader from Siam marched up to be baptized!

Being christened meant the natives had to choose Christian names. Humabon wanted to be called Charles, after the king of Spain.

In the following days, though, Ferdinand was surprised to see that **the idols were still there**. He even found dozens hidden away in Humabon's own home. And when he came upon some islanders making offerings to the figures, he demanded an explanation.

The natives explained that they were making offerings on behalf of a man who had been too sick to be baptized.

Ferdinand marched everyone to the sick man's house and found him lying motionless. But when the chaplain baptized the man . . . he suddenly became well! In his diary, Pigafetta described it as a miracle. But was it?

After that, according to Pigafetta, Ferdinand made the islanders take all their figures to the beach and burn them. We don't know how the natives felt about burning their precious figures, but we can guess.

As for Ferdinand . . . he now had a new ambition.

10 FERDINAND IS FAMOUS (FINALLY)

Some of the other islanders disapproved of the burning of idols. Several chieftains refused to pay tribute to King Charles. Not only that, they weren't interested in being baptized.

On the island of Mactan, chieftain Lapu Lapu told everyone to ignore the Europeans. **Ferdinand was outraged.** Lapu Lapu was way less important than Humabon, and Mactan was tiny compared to Cebu. How could he be so rude? That Lapu Lapu needed to be taught a lesson!

Ferdinand assembled a detachment of men and sent them to Mactan, where they burned down a village and planted a cross in its smoldering ruins.

But a few days later, Ferdinand was outraged again. A chieftain named Sula turned up to deliver his tribute to King Charles . . . and it was just two goats! Realizing how offended Ferdinand was, Sula told him that Lapu Lapu had been warning everyone not to pay tribute to the king of Spain and had forbidden Sula from taking more than two goats!

Lapu Lapu made me do it!

The old Ferdinand would have weighed Sula's words carefully. He would have wondered whether the chieftain was just trying to get himself out of trouble by blaming someone who wasn't in the room. But the new Ferdinand was a bit of a fanatic; he saw himself not as a guest of the islanders but as their conqueror.

This was his chance to show off Europe's military might! He told Sula he was going to send three longboats of men to show Lapu Lapu *"how the Spanish lions fight."*

And he was going to lead them himself.

INTO BATTLE

Everyone tried to persuade Ferdinand not to go. Even Pigafetta, who always agreed with his master, thought it was reckless. Besides, their mission had been to get to the Spice Islands, and they still hadn't managed it! But Ferdinand wouldn't listen.

At dawn on April 27, 1521, the fleet anchored in the deep water off Mactan. All around them the boats of Rajah Humabon and his men dotted the channel. Ferdinand had invited them to watch—this was going to be **another magnificent display of power**.

Three longboats were lowered into the sea. Ferdinand took forty-eight men in all, including

Pigafetta and Enrique. They were all dressed in armored breastplates and helmets.

The tide was on the turn and the water was too shallow for the longboats to get close to the shore. **The men had to climb out of the boats into the water**, which was thigh high, and wade nearly half a mile to shore in their heavy gear.

Ferdinand expected to be outnumbered but he was confident his guns and crossbows would easily defeat native weapons. He was taken aback, though, when warriors suddenly charged out of the jungle with bloodcurdling cries.

In all, there were around 1,500 of them running toward Ferdinand and his men, wielding stones and mud, iron-tipped spears, poisoned arrows, and pointed stakes hardened in the flames of a fire.

Ferdinand's crossbowmen and gunners began shooting immediately, but their missiles couldn't stop the advancing enemy. **The island warriors knew exactly where to aim:** straight at the Europeans' unarmored legs! Ferdinand's regular demonstrations of the armor's strength had also taught everyone its weakness.

The Europeans managed to scramble past their attackers and into a village set in a grove of palm trees. "Burn their houses!" Ferdinand commanded. "Terrify them!'

His men raced through the village, setting fire to twenty or thirty huts . . . but then more warriors appeared. Realizing that they were being overwhelmed, Ferdinand called for a retreat. Everyone hastily waded back into the sea, heading for the longboats, but it was too late. Many of his men fell around him as Ferdinand battled for more than an hour, knee deep in water. Soon only seven men were left fighting alongside him, including Pigafetta and Enrique.

Pigafetta saw that an arrow was protruding from Ferdinand's right leg. He watched as Ferdinand parried a bamboo spear, then killed the man who'd thrown it, but as he tried to draw his sword, a spear wounded his arm. Ferdinand was growing weaker by the moment and Pigafetta realized that **the arrow in his leg was poisoned**.

Ferdinand stumbled and the enemy warriors swarmed around him. *"They rushed upon him with iron and bamboo spears and with their cutlasses,"* Pigafetta wrote sadly in his diary. *"They killed our mirror, our light, our comfort and our true guide."*

While Pigafetta's words were loving, it was clear that day that **the other Europeans did not share his feelings**.

The men guarding the longboats in the shallows had stayed where they were. They made no move to help those trapped on the shore. Neither had the officers and men watching from the three ships—they hadn't fired their cannons when the trouble began. Humabon had been observing from a boat offshore, but he waited until he saw Ferdinand fall before his men went to the Europeans' aid.

NUMB

Humabon's men rescued the survivors and ferried them back to the Spanish ships.

Pigafetta survived. So did Enrique, but they were badly wounded and numbed by Ferdinand's death. They were surprised when the officers swiftly organized an election to choose who would take over from Ferdinand as commander. It was as if they'd known Ferdinand wasn't going to make it . . .

In fact, when they returned to Cebu, the men who'd stayed to continue trading were **all packed up**, as if they'd known they'd be leaving soon. Indeed, the newly appointed officers were determined to sail away as soon as possible. According to Pigafetta, they needed Enrique to deliver a message to the king first (though we don't know what the message was).

But Enrique wouldn't do it. He had taken to his bed.

From his own sickbed, Pigafetta listened as the new officers ordered Enrique to get up. Enrique refused. He was a free man, he told them, now that Ferdinand was dead; he didn't have to follow orders anymore.

Ferdinand's death meant that **he had failed** in his mission. He was never going to return to Spain . . . and none of the money he had left in his will was going to reach his family. The *San Antonio* had docked in Spain a few days after the battle, and Archbishop Fonseca—

on learning what Ferdinand had done to his son, Cartagena—stopped paying Ferdinand's salary to his wife. Only one of Ferdinand's wishes could be fulfilled . . . that Enrique should be freed.

But the new officers were having none of it. They insisted that Enrique was still a slave and **threatened to whip him** if he didn't follow their orders. So, Enrique had no choice but to obey.

ONE LAST BANQUET

Humabon invited the Europeans to one last banquet, and a large group went ashore for the party, including the newly elected officers, who forced Enrique to come with them. Normally, Pigafetta would have gone along, but he'd been wounded by a poisoned arrow to the forehead, so he stayed on the ship.

Not long afterward, he heard shouting. He joined the others on deck to find several of the men who'd gone to the party swimming toward the ships. In the distance, they could hear horrifying screams. The survivors said Humabon's warriors had emerged from the shadows and attacked them as they sat at the feast. **Twenty-seven Europeans were killed.** Father Valderrama and one of the ships' pilots had been taken prisoner.

In a panic, the three ships raised anchor and

prepared to leave, even though Humabon still held a handful of their men. Looking back at the shore, they could see the islanders pulling down a cross that Ferdinand had erected and **smashing it to pieces**.

What had turned Humabon against the Europeans? Perhaps Enrique had told him about how Europeans behaved. Perhaps Humabon himself had plotted with Lapu Lapu to rid the islands of the boastful foreigner who had forced them to burn the idols they worshipped.

Maybe Humabon had just had enough of being hospitable to an invader.

The Journey Continues Without Ferdinand

Leaving Ferdinand's body behind and abandoning the European prisoners to their fate on the island, the fleet sailed on. Without Ferdinand's leadership and skill, they **bickered and struggled** and made things up as they went along, still hoping to find the Moluccas. Pigafetta, who was maybe feeling lonely without Ferdinand's support, tried to keep out of everyone's way but carried on recording the journey in his diary.

With only 115 crewmen left out of the original 260, there weren't enough people to sail all three ships. So, they burned the *Concepción* and split the men and provisions between the *Trinidad* and the *Victoria*.

PIGAFETTA'S DIARY

We started sailing south, without knowing where we were going.

1. We sailed away from Cebu.
2. A friendly king at Cipit gave us supplies.
3. At Palawan, we kidnapped another ship's pilot to direct us to Borneo.
4. We stayed on beautiful Borneo for 35 days and even rode elephants!

5. In Cimbonbon, we stopped for repairs and saw leaves that walked!*
6. We raided a boat for 20 hogs, 20 goats, 150 chickens, and more!
7. In Sarangani, we captured two native pilots who showed us the way.
8. Weaving through lots of tiny islands, some prisoners escaped.
9. Tidore at last!

Well, we're here!

Finally, six months after Ferdinand's death, they landed in the Moluccas.

* They were actually insects that looked like leaves!

The two ships had finally reached their destination! But they quickly discovered that Ferdinand's cousin Francisco Serrão was dead, and the Portuguese were still hunting down Magellan as a traitor. They had to load up with spices and get away—fast!

Then, just as they were about to leave, the *Trinidad* sprang a leak. While it stayed behind for repairs, the *Victoria* sailed on alone. It was **a 10,000-mile journey** that would take them through forbidden territory that the pope had given to the Portuguese.

THE JOURNEY HOME

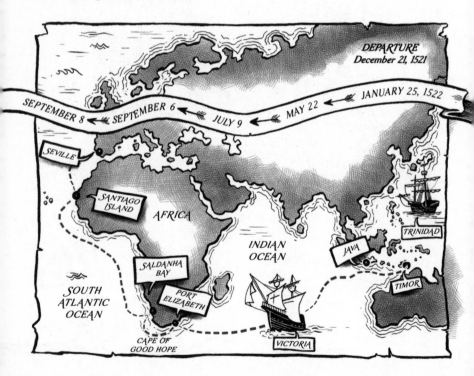

On the journey, the ship lost many men: scurvy struck again, there were accidental deaths, and a few men deserted. By the journey's end, **only eighteen men remained** out of the sixty who'd set off from the Spice Islands. The ship finally entered the Guadalquivir River on September 10, 1522. It was leaking badly and towed by a smaller boat, but the fragrance of their cargo filled the harbor. The ship was carrying an astonishing 381 sacks of cloves—the best-quality cloves anyone in Seville had ever seen.

And the man who had captained the ship on this last stage of the voyage? He was none other than **Juan Sebastián Elcano**, who had been part of one of the most serious mutinies against Ferdinand. You'd think he should have been worried about returning to Spain!

Well, he had no need to be. King Charles, who was still short on money, was thrilled by the fortune he made from the cloves. He invited Elcano to his palace and granted him an annual pension, a knighthood, and a coat of arms. And, after an investigation, Elcano was even pardoned for his part in the mutiny.

Meanwhile, where was Ferdinand's ship, the *Trinidad*? Well, the good news is the crew survived. The bad news is they ran into the Portuguese and were **put in jail**. Spain had to negotiate for their freedom.

FERDINAND'S NAME

Ferdinand dreamed he would be remembered as one of the greatest explorers of all time. But that wasn't the way it happened in 1522. He was hated in Portugal for renouncing King Manuel, and in Spain, King Charles's support had infuriated a lot of important people. To make matters worse, nine days after Ferdinand was killed, the *San Antonio* and its mutinous crew had made it back to Seville on May 6, 1521. The men **told a bunch of lies** about Ferdinand. They claimed:

❈ Ferdinand was a secret Portuguese agent

❈ That he was planning to dupe the king

❈ That he had tortured Spanish officers (true) for no good reason (not true)

Then, when Elcano was called for questioning, he blamed everything bad that had happened on Ferdinand too.

It's all absolutely true!

None of Ferdinand's meticulous diaries of the voyage were ever recovered. Perhaps they were destroyed by the survivors who didn't want the king to discover the truth?

It seemed the only person who wasn't out to ruin Ferdinand's name was Pigafetta, who promptly sat down and wrote an account of the voyage from his journal, with **Ferdinand starring as its noble hero**. His account avoided mentioning the mutinies and Ferdinand's harsh punishments—he probably didn't want to attract the vengeance of the survivors. Pigafetta then traveled between royal courts, from Spain to Portugal to France to Venice, telling his story.

Ferdinand's family had been hit hard by the voyage. Poor Beatriz, Ferdinand's wife, had lost the baby she was carrying when the fleet set out, and their young son, Rodrigo, died from illness. Ferdinand had taken Beatriz's brother, Duarte Barbosa, and his illegitimate son, Cristóvão Rebelo, along for the adventure. Barbosa was killed during that last fatal banquet in Cebu, while Rebelo died at his father's side during the battle of Mactan. Records don't tell us what happened to Diogo, Ferdinand's brother.

All his life, Ferdinand had yearned for recognition but was thwarted at every turn. Today, thanks to Pigafetta, everyone agrees **his epic voyage was an extraordinary achievement**. Ferdinand Magellan is credited as the first man to circumnavigate the world, even though he didn't actually make it before he died. It was his fleet—or what was left of it—that finished

the journey. Some say the honor should
go to Elcano.

But if Enrique spoke the language of Cebu, he must
have lived on that island before Ferdinand found him
in Malacca. So . . . **Enrique might actually have been
the first man to circumnavigate the world!**

Whatever the truth may be, Ferdinand's name
continued to be remembered for many things:

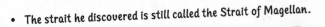

- The strait he discovered is still called the Strait of Magellan.

- He discovered the Magellanic Clouds, which are
  actually galaxies.

- The "black geese" the crew found are
  now called Magellanic penguins.

- Early maps called South America
  Magellanica or Magellanic Land.

- For many years, the ocean that Ferdinand had named the Pacific
  was called the Sea of Magellan.

Ferdinand set out to find spices. What he discovered instead was a world that was bigger than anyone had realized.

EPILOGUE

The Age of Exploration transformed Europe. Along with the spices, explorers also brought completely new foods to Europe: potatoes, chocolate, tomatoes, pineapples, peanuts, vanilla . . . They realized the true size of the Earth, mapped the oceans and many of the continents, and they revolutionized world trade. Small countries like Spain and Portugal became world powers. To this day, Europe still enjoys the profits of the Age of Exploration.

But for the people they met on their adventures, it was a time of invasion:

- ✺ They were attacked and had their wealth and land stolen.
- ✺ They were enslaved in unbelievable numbers for centuries, because of the Europeans' technology and advanced seafaring know-how.
- ✺ Hundreds of thousands were killed by European diseases they'd never been exposed to before.

The Age of Exploration was a time when people all over the world realized that they were not alone.

While Europeans found untold wealth in the new places they discovered, **the locals were robbed** of their land and possessions. To them the Age of Exploration was more like the Age of Exploitation.

THE AGE OF ~~EXPLORATION~~ Exploitation

Americas
95% of indigenous people here were killed by European diseases after the Age of Exploration.

The Philippines and the Mariana Islands
Both were ruled by Spain for more than 300 years. The Philippines is now the third largest Catholic country in the world.

India
India endured colonial rule by the Portuguese, the Dutch, the French, the Danish, the Norwegians, and the British.

NORTH AMERICA

SPAIN
PORTUGAL EUROPE

INDIA

AFRICA

SOUTH AMERICA

ATLANTIC OCEAN

INDIAN OCEAN

Africa
The Atlantic Slave Trade, started by Portugal's Henry the Navigator, transported 12 million Africans to the Caribbean and North America.

The Spice Islands
In the 1600s, the Dutch and Portuguese battled over the Spice Islands, killing thousands of islanders. Eventually, other countries began to grow spices, and the Spice Islands lost their attraction to Europeans.

TIMELINE

Here you are! A handy list of all my amazing achievements!

1490
Ferdinand becomes an orphan.

1493
Christopher Columbus's ship blows into Lisbon harbor, and he thinks he's just sailed to China and back.

| 1490

| 1495

1480
Ferdinand Magellan is born in Sabrosa, Portugal.

1494
The pope agrees a treaty dividing the New World in two—half for Spain and half for Portugal!

1495
King John II of Portugal dies, and King Manuel the Fortunate takes the throne.

1498
Vasco da Gama lands in Calicut, India. He is the first explorer to travel around the southern tip of Africa to India.

1504
King Manuel sends six armadas to the Indian Ocean. They attack and loot other ships and raid settlements in Africa and India.

| 1500

| 1505

1505
Ferdinand signs up to Manuel's Seventh India Armada.

1509
Ferdinand fights in the Battle of Diu, India. The Portuguese finally beat the Moors.

1513
Ferdinand returns to Portugal a war hero—but finds he is penniless.

| 1510

| 1515

1517
In despair, Ferdinand leaves Portugal for Spain.

September 10, 1519
Ferdinand leaves Seville for the
Spice Islands with five ships and
over 235 crew, funded by King
Charles I of Spain.

October 1519
A first attempted mutiny
against Ferdinand fails.

April 1, 1520
A second mutiny
attempt fails.

| 1520

December 29, 1519
The armada reaches
the South American
coast.

May 22, 1520
Ferdinand's smallest
ship, the *Santiago*, is
wrecked.

October 18, 1520
Ferdinand finds
the strait.

October 28, 1520
Ferdinand sends
the *San Antonio* on
an errand. It turns
around and heads
back to Spain.

April 27, 1521
Ferdinand is killed by
warriors on Mactan
Island.

| 1520

| 1521

November 28, 1520
The armada
eventually emerges
from the strait into
a big new ocean: the
Pacific.

March 6, 1521
After more than three
months at sea, the armada
arrives at previously
uncharted Guam.

March 16, 1521
They land in the Philippines.

May 6, 1521
The *San Antonio* and its mutinous crew get to Seville and start telling lies about Ferdinand.

| 1522 | 1523

November 6, 1521
After six months wandering around the East Indies, what's left of the armada reaches the Spice Islands!

September 10, 1522
The lone surviving ship, the *Victoria*, docks at Seville with a tiny crew but tons of valuable spices.

You see, I was right all along!

GLOSSARY

Age of Exploration: Also known as the "Age of Discovery." It was a time when Europeans searched for new routes around the world. It stretched from the mid-15th century to the mid-16th century.

Arab: A person who comes from Arabia or other parts of the Middle East. In Ferdinand's time, Europeans randomly referred to people of color as Arabs, Indians, or Moors.

armada : A large group of ships armed for battle.

banquet: A big, fancy dinner or feast.

barnacle: A tiny sea creature with a shell that sticks to docks, rocks, and the bottoms of ships.

barren: Land where crops are unable to grow.

blacksmith: Somebody who shapes iron into objects, using fire and a hammer.

cape: A large point of land that sticks out into the sea.

circumnavigate: To travel all the way around.

clan: A group of people who share the same ancestors.

colony: A place occupied and controlled by people from another country.

commerce: The business of buying and selling goods, services, and trade.

conquer: To overcome or take by force.

courtier: A member of a royal court.

diplomat: Someone whose job is to handle relations with other countries' governments.

empire: A group of countries ruled by the same leader or government.

fencing: The sport of sword fighting.

fleet: A group of ships.

forge: Move forward gradually but steadily.

galaxy: A collection of billions of stars, gas, and dust particles held together by gravity. Earth is in the Milky Way galaxy.

hawking: Training a bird of prey to hunt.

hemisphere: One of two halves of the Earth. The planet can be divided into the northern and southern or eastern and western hemispheres.

idyllic: Peaceful, simple, and natural.

Indian: Someone from India. In Ferdinand's time, Europeans randomly referred to people of color as Arabs, Indians, or Moors.

indigenous: Original population of a particular country or area.

ironwood: Trees that produce very hard, heavy wood.

146

lavish: Luxurious and expensive.

lieutenant: A military officer.

loot: To take valuable items by force.

Mamluk: A Muslim ruler who was originally a slave.

maravedi: Old Spanish coins made from copper or gold.

medieval: Relating to the Middle Ages (from roughly 500—1500).

monsoon: Seasonal, strong winds, usually accompanied by lots of heavy rain.

Moor: A Muslim. In Ferdinand's time, Europeans randomly referred to people of color as Arabs, Indians, or Moors.

mutiny: Rebellion of soldiers or sailors against the officers in charge of them.

New World: In the 16th century, North and South America were known as the New World.

Ottoman Empire: A large, Islamic empire that grew out of Turkey and lasted over 600 years. During the 15th and 16th centuries, it was one of the world's most powerful states.

page: A boy employed as a servant to a knight.

pamphlet: A thin book with a paper cover, giving information on a particular topic.

pension: Money a person can live on after retiring from work.

Persia: The country known as Iran today.

plunder: To steal from someone using force.

reef: To gather in the sails of a ship, e.g. during high winds.

sabotage: To deliberately damage or destroy something, often for political reasons.

scoundrel: Someone who is dishonest or lacks honor.

seafaring: Traveling by sea.

settlement: A place where a group of people have chosen to live.

stocks: A wooden device that closed over the hands and feet of criminals to punish and humiliate them.

sultan: Historical ruler of an Islamic country.

trafficking: Buying and selling.

uncharted: Not recorded on any map.

vet: To check how good something is.

vineyard: An area where grapes are grown to make wine.

yardarm: The outer ends of a horizontal pole in the rigging of a ship).

NOTES

60 "would go . . . by the Portuguese": Samuel Eliot Morison, *Admiral of the Ocean Sea*. New York: Little, Brown, 1991 (reissue edition); page 319.

70 "The masters . . . loved him not": Antonio Pigafetta, *Magellan's Voyage: A Narrative Account of the First Circumnavigation*, trans. R. A. Skelton. New York: Dover Publications, 1961; page 38.

86 "He had a very . . . two hearts painted": Pigfetta, *Magellan's Voyage*; page 47.

100 "Several small stars . . . clouds of mist": Pigfetta, *Magellan's Voyage*; page 58.

101 "The Moluccas . . . appointed place!": Laurence Bergeen, *Over the Edge of the World: Magellan's Terrifying Circumnavigation of the Globe*. New York: William Morrow, 2003; page 92.

101 "I believe that . . . a voyage": Pigfetta, *Magellan's Voyage*; page 57.

103 "They were . . . to fly": Bergeen, *Over the Edge of the World*; page 94.

118 "Treat them . . . for you": Pigfetta, *Magellan's Voyage*; page 75.

122 "how . . . lions fight": Pigfetta, *Magellan's Voyage*; page 56.

125 "They rushed . . . their cutlasses": Pigfetta, *Magellan's Voyage*; page 88.

125 "They killed . . . true guide": Pigfetta, *Magellan's Voyage*; page 88.

134 "All who . . . rendered speechless": Bergeen, *Over the Edge of the World*; page 272.

Select Bibliography

Bergeen, Laurence. *Over the Edge of the World: Magellan's Terrifying Circumnavigation of the Globe*. New York: William Morrow, 2003.

Morison, Samuel Eliot. *Admiral of the Ocean Sea* (reissue edition). New York: Little, Brown, 1991.

Pigafetta, Antonio. *Magellan's Voyage: A Narrative Account of the First Circumnavigation* (trans. R. A. Skelton). New York: Dover Publications, 1961.

INDEX

Use these pages for a quick reference!

150

This book should have been about me!

GET ON A FIRST-NAME
BASIS WITH ALL THESE
FAMOUS FIGURES!

THE FIRST
NAMES SERIES

first names

HARRY Houdini

"Be with you in a minute!"

Kjartan Poskitt ★ Illustrated by Geraint Ford

first names

AMELIA Earhart

"For me, it was love at first flight!"

Andrew Prentice ★ Illustrated by Mike Smith

first names

NOBEL PEACE PRIZE 2014

MALALA Yousafzai

SCHOOL

NO GIRLS

"Don't tell me I can't go to school!"

Lisa Williamson ★ Illustrated by Mike Smith

first names

Beep!

ADA Lovelace

"I dreamed up computer programming!"

Ben Jeapes ★ Illustrated by Nick Ward

ABOUT THE AUTHOR

Candy Gourlay is an author and journalist who has known that she wanted to write ever since she was a little girl in the Philippines. She lives in London with her husband and her three children.

ABOUT THE ILLUSTRATOR

Tom Knight is an illustrator and writer. He lives in England with his wife, Tabby, and his two sons, Archie and Seth.